Peter Burwash's
Vegetarian Primer

Peter Burwash's

Vegetarian Primer

BY

PETER BURWASH

AND

JOHN TULLIUS

Atheneum

NEW YORK

1983

Library of Congress Cataloging in Publication Data

Burwash, Peter.
  Peter Burwash's Vegetarian primer.

  Bibliography: p.
  Includes index.
  1. Vegetarianism. 2. Vegetarian cookery. I. Tullius,
John. II. Title. III. Title: Vegetarian primer.
TX392.B78 1983   641.5′636   82-45165
ISBN 0-689-11299-8

Published simultaneously in Canada by McClelland and Stewart Ltd.
Composition by American–Stratford Graphic Services, Inc.,
Brattleboro, Vermont
Manufactured by Fairfield Graphics, Fairfield, Pennsylvania
Designed by Kathleen Carey
First Edition

TO BERNARD GUSMAN

whose initial research motivated and inspired this book

Acknowledgments

Thanks to Cindy Wachholz, Tom Dyer, Monika Dinoffer, Joe Dinoffer, Vikki Rovai, Mary Ann Rovai, and H. B. Laski for their generous assistance in putting together the final manuscript.

A very special expression of gratitude to Chris Reid and Shannon Robinson who did all of the heavy editing and re-working of several drafts of this book—and also for putting up with the authors.

Thank you to Lou Ann Runyan, whose beautiful illustrations accompany this book. Lou Ann believed in our idea and was generous enough to offer her talents for what we could afford.

Finally, thanks to a certain doctor on a beach in Waikiki, who opened my eyes.

Introduction

Peter Burwash and I first met on a tennis court. I was un-
lucky enough to draw him as an opponent in the first
round of a tournament in Hawaii. Since he was a world-
class player and I was not, since he'd played Davis Cup
for Canada, was their number one player in 1971 and
ranked number one in Hawaii in 1973, 1975, and 1977, I
knew I was going to lose the match. What I expected was
a spectacular display of shots and strategy that would
wipe me off the court posthaste, without much adieu,
thank you very much. But that didn't happen. Oh, I lost
in quick order, to be sure. But instead of great tennis,
what beat me, what, in fact, overwhelmed me, was an un-
believable display of energy. Burwash would run down
every ball, climb the fence to retrieve an overhead, dive
for balls (on concrete courts!), roll, get up, dive again, and
hit a winner. He barely worked up a sweat, wasn't
breathing hard, and throughout the match had an eager,
bouncing, indefatigable energy that absolutely poured
from him. I had to know how he did it.

Peter Burwash is easily the busiest and most productive

man I've ever met. He sleeps three hours a day—four if he's feeling overworked. For the last four years he has averaged two million air miles per year. He is president of Peter Burwash International, the largest international network of tennis professionals in the world, staffing about a hundred of the most prestigious tennis clubs and resorts on five continents—in Tokyo, Munich, Lahaina (Maui), Houston, and on and on. PBI also runs international programs for the blind and the handicapped, and began the International Foundation of Wheelchair Tennis, and a nationwide tennis program for prisoners.

Peter tours some two hundred days a year with The Peter Burwash International Tennis Show, which has been described as the Harlem Globetrotters of tennis, and is ninety minutes of tennis instruction, entertainment, music, juggling, ball tricks, and a constant barrage of laugh-makers designed to send you away a better tennis player. The Tennis Show has performed in ninety-one countries, every Canadian province, and all fifty states, for Prince Rainier in Monte Carlo, for the Emperor of Japan's birthday in the Tokyo National Stadium, and for the last three years at the U.S. Open Tennis Championships for CBS. But Peter has also taken his show to every frontier of tennis—to Micronesia, where the natives played bare-breasted, and to Malawi, East Africa, where he arrived in a small, single-engine plane and set up a tennis court (net and all) right on the dirt runway. The local folks, none of whom had even seen a tennis racket, came literally out of the jungle first to gawk and then to play.

In between all this he keeps up a prodigious tour of speaking engagements. He's been the featured speaker at just about every important tennis teachers' conference, including the USTA National Tennis Teachers' Conference held in New York every year during the fortnight of the U.S. Open. He's also, of course, deeply involved in health and vegetarianism and, therefore, year after year has been a featured speaker at most of the important health and vegetarian gatherings worldwide—including the National Health Federation, the North American Vegetarian Conference and the World Vegetarian Conference.

By now you're probably asking yourself the same question I asked Peter that first day—"Where does one human being get all that energy?" His answer led eventually to this book.

JOHN TULLIUS

Contents

Contents

Contents

PART FOUR: Going Vegetarian
Phase One: The Nutritional Concerns

PART FIVE: Going Vegetarian
Phase Two: Making Your Vegetarian Diet Work

PART SIX: Vegetarianism and the Athlete

Contents

PART SEVEN: Vegetarian Recipes

PART EIGHT: Bibliography

Part One

THE VEGETARIAN FUGITIVE

Becoming a Fugitive

One day in 1971, when I had a few days off between tennis circuits, I was throwing a Frisbee around on the beach in Waikiki with a bunch of my friends and accidentally hit a guy on the head with the Frisbee. I went over to apologize, and it turned out he was a doctor who was in town attending a medical symposium on diets—the essence of which was that meat was the worst thing you could put in your body. Oh, no! Vegetarians!

It was one of those perfect days with just a scatter of clouds sliding by, a cool trade wind gently blowing, and the waves slowly arcing up and dropping in beautiful rhythm. I remember thinking as I sat there talking with this doctor, "Geez, I'd love to get back to the Frisbee." But I felt obliged to sit there and listen to this guy because I'd bopped him on the head.

I have always tried to live by the idea that an intelligent person has an open mind, because a closed-minded person learns nothing. But, to tell the truth, I had a preconceived notion of a vegetarian as a kind of scrawny know-it-all. Vegetarianism was totally foreign to me. Born and raised in Toronto, Canada, I was brought up as a hockey player and my whole conditioning concerning food was through hockey. A big, juicy steak was a reward and preparation for battle all at once.

I played collegiate hockey for the University of Toronto, and right after hockey practice every night the big event was sitting around the training table. We all had our choice of steaks and the chef knew me well because I would only allow him to cook mine fifteen to twenty seconds on each side. I wanted it raw—just dripping blood.

There would always be steak, potatoes, and an assortment of vegetables on the menu each night. In three years of playing hockey six nights a week, September through April, at all those dinners I never once ate the vegetables. I couldn't stand vegetables. I had to take a bite and wash them down with a drink of water. The only reason I ever ate vegetables at all was because I heard they were good for you.

So every night at the training table I had this big splat of instant mashed potatoes with gravy. See, I always had the gravy because I had been told that the gravy was the blood drippings and the blood of the animal was the best thing for you. So that was my meal—a corpse cooked fifteen seconds on each side and potatoes mixed with blood!

One of the first questions a person interested in vegetarianism will ask is, "What will I eat?" So I ask them, "Do you eat fruits?" "Oh, sure, I really enjoy fruits." "Do you eat vegetables?" "Oh, yeah, I love 'em." "How about spaghetti?" "Oh, I love Italian food." And I go on and on and they find out they really love vegetarian foods. They just didn't know it.

But there I was. I mean, I hated vegetables. I wouldn't go near anything green. It just wasn't my color. And here's this doctor telling me I couldn't eat meat or fish or poultry or eggs or anything like that. So, of course, I really didn't want to listen to him because he wanted to take away the only things I enjoyed eating. I was not interested in eating fruits and vegetables because, at that moment, at twenty-five years of age, I had never eaten a salad.

What first caught my curiosity, though, was when the doctor said an athlete shouldn't eat meat six months before an event. Then he went on to support that statement by drawing diagrams of the intestines and charts of the tooth structures of vegetarian animals versus carnivores—right there in the sand. Finally, he convinced me I should show up at the symposium.

But I needed a little moral support, so I went with seven friends—five guys and two girls. We showed up at the Hilton Hawaiian Village Convention Center, where there were 300 doctors, all in suits and ties. In come eight beach bums in bare feet and bathing suits, hauling surfboards that we propped up against the wall so we could get out of there fast. I mean, this was an infringement on my beach time. I had ten days' break from the professional tennis circuits I was playing then, and those ten days were my only time off all year. Three days later I had to fly to New Zealand. So we all made a deal that as soon as it got boring, we'd head back to the beach. Total estimated time we expected to stay there was about five minutes.

Well, five *hours* later, after dozens of speakers and demonstrations and statistics and studies and tests, we finally left. I went "cold turkey" off meat that day and haven't touched a piece of meat, fish, poultry, or an egg since. That's how convinced I was.

I remember walking back down to the beach afterward and thinking to myself, "I'm a vegetarian! I'm never going to eat meat again." The only problem was, what *was* I going to eat? I hated vegetables. And when the reality hit of just exactly *what* I was going to eat and *where* I was going to eat, I panicked. I was in Hawaii. They've got bananas and papayas but I hated fruit—so that was out. Also, I was living in a hotel and back in the early '70's there were few vegetarian restaurants to speak of. All you could get at hotels and restaurants were vegetables boiled into mush. So my diet became French fries, spaghetti, and grilled-cheese sandwiches.

But, even with all the junk food, I felt terrific on and off the court for the first three months. The immediate effects were exhilarating. I felt lighter and quicker, and I had an amazing burst of energy and speed. I jumped out of bed at dawn. Before, my scenario was to go to bed at midnight and get up at noon—if the alarm went off. Otherwise, I'd sleep all day if I could. All of a sudden, I was up every morning at seven o'clock.

Then the withdrawals hit me.

No one had explained to me about the withdrawal period that might occur.

About four months into the program I was in a tournament in Richmond, Virginia, standing on the baseline getting ready to return a serve, and my uppermost priority at that moment was to stay on my feet. All of a sudden the court started listing as if I were on a boat in rough seas. As long as I was moving there was no dizziness. But for one entire month, every time I stood still, I felt dizzy. I'd be standing in the crowded aisle of an airplane waiting to get off and I'd feel like falling over. Or, when I was teaching tennis, I had to teach holding onto the net post or kneeling down. Throughout this period I felt extremely weak and it was a supreme effort to get out of bed each morning.

I was a very heavy meat-eater, so I was destined for a very heavy withdrawal. Unfortunately, I didn't know how to deal with it. Anyone who understands the vitamins and food supplements that may be necessary during the transition period doesn't often experience these extreme withdrawal problems.

On top of my withdrawal symptoms, as is usual with a new vegetarian, I was receiving a lot of criticism from family, friends, people I met—everyone! On the tennis circuit I was always being razzed by the other players because athletes are, by and large, a very conservative bunch. Anything out of the routine is immediately suspect.

I remember Marty Riessen, with whom I played doubles in South Africa, once yelling out at me from the stands after I missed a ball, "Hey, Burwash, you'd be a lot faster if you didn't have so many carrots hanging out of your ears." And Riessen was one of the nice guys!

Then there was the day I returned to my home in Canada for the summer circuit. And the moment I walked in the door, my mother—who is a very giving, caring person—said, "Look what we've got for you!" and showed me this big, bloody cut of beef. See, she knew that was the meal I loved the most—my corpse-and-mashed-potato-and-blood diet.

I didn't have the heart to tell her right then and there that I was now a vegetarian. It wasn't until later that evening, as she was making dinner and had the meat unwrapped and was actually about to put it on the fire, that I spilled the beans. For a long time after that my mother constantly worried that I was going to shrivel up and die. My father, however, took it all a little more in stride. He just figured I'd flipped.

That's when I became a "vegetarian fugitive." For one entire year, I refused to discuss my eating habits with anyone. My parents thought I'd gone off the deep end, many of the players on the circuit constantly ribbed me, and most of my friends wondered if I'd ever be well again.

Then, suddenly, one day everything just cleared up and I was never again bothered by withdrawal symptoms. Once again I felt a terrific sense of well-being both on and off the court.

Now came the incident that convinced me beyond any doubt that I was on the right road. Every year I had been going to Lloyd Percival's Fitness Center in Toronto,

7

where Lloyd had a program in which he tested all of the top athletes in Canada. From 1968 to 1970, when I was still a meat-eater, I was between number fifty and number sixty in the country.

The year I stopped eating meat, I really wanted to do well in the test. I had to at least score in the top sixty again so I wouldn't look like a complete idiot—but the cards were stacked against me. The day before the test, I had to play in the finals of a tournament in St. Petersburg, Florida. Billie Jean King and Chris Evert were in the women's final right before me, and they had a long match. Then I got into a long match myself and missed my plane for Toronto. Finally I got a late plane to Cleveland and ended up sleeping overnight on a bench at the Hopkins Airport in Cleveland with my tennis bag for a pillow. The next morning I caught a 7 A.M. flight to Toronto. When I got off the plane in Toronto I went straight to the Fitness Center, and I felt the way anyone would feel if they'd slept all night on a bench in an airport—totally exhausted. The testing procedure ahead of me was twelve hours long.

About halfway through the testing, a doctor came rushing into the room and said, "What have you been doing?" And, of course, the first thing that went through my head was, "Aw, geez, I don't want to hear it!" I didn't care what this guy said, or what the tests said, or what anyone said—I was not giving up. By this time I'd taken flak from everyone for a year and now it was going to be proved *scientifically* that I was a fool.

8

No, I did not want to hear it!

But then the doctor said, "You've improved 38% in your left arm strength, and 52% in your oxygen uptake, and 40% in this area, and 80% in that area." And on and on. I'd figured here was another guy who was going to give me static about being a vegetarian and suddenly he was giving me proof I'd been right all along.

Picture it. My resting pulse is being taken, so I'm lying flat on my back with my palms up and I'm supposed to be in a completely relaxed state with my mind cleared of all thought, and in comes this doctor telling me I'm not nuts after all. So I jumped up with a big smile on my face which, of course, immediately fouled up all the pulse readings. But, heck, I didn't care. After a year of being a Vegetarian Fugitive, those were sweet words.

Then about ten minutes later all of the doctors at the institute came in and started grilling me:

"What have you been eating?"

"What kind of food?"

"How much chicken and fish?"

So I explained what a vegetarian was, and that there are three basic types of vegetarians, and that I was a lacto-vegetarian. Here I was just your average meat-and-potatoes-and-blood man just one year before, and now I'm educating a battery of doctors.

It was a strange scene but the evidence was irrefutable. I had significantly improved my score in every area tested. I wasn't training. I didn't run. I'd just been playing my regular tournament tennis schedule, and I was traveling a lot, which is a great strain on the body. The only change in life-style I had made was my diet. After one year as a vegetarian I had the highest fitness index of any athlete in the country, and I remained number one every year I was tested.

9

The Myth of Vegetarianism

There is an illusion surrounding vegetarianism, a wall of ignorance, that is centuries thick. I like to call it the "myth of vegetarianism." I have given thousands of lectures on health and vegetarianism, and after these lectures I am usually surrounded by people eagerly asking questions. I've found that, even in today's increasingly health-conscious world, most people are totally ignorant of the most basic facts about vegetarianism.

For example, whenever I speak to a large group of people I always ask them to define vegetarianism. The replies inevitably deal with the eating of vegetables. That's logical, but wrong. The word vegetarian does not derive from the word "vegetable," but from the Latin word *vegitore* which means "whole, sound, fresh, or lively."

Most people also assume that a vegetarian is just a person who eats vegetables. In fact, the word vegetarian covers a wide range of eating habits. There are many types of vegetarians (I've seen a list of as many as 200 different permutations!), but the three most common types, making up 95 percent of all vegetarians, are vegans, lacto-vegetarians, and lacto-ovo-vegetarians.

Vegans eat only grains, legumes, nuts, fruits, and vegetables. Lacto-vegetarians follow a vegan diet but include dairy products such as milk, cheese, and butter. A lacto-ovo-vegetarian eats what a lacto-vegetarian eats but also includes eggs in the diet.

One of the most widely accepted myths about vegetarians is that they are a bunch of scrawny weirdos who carry around bags of nuts and eat a lot of seaweed—in a word, "health nuts." Being concerned about your health doesn't seem particularly crazy to me. In fact, it seems rather insane not to care.

Those who discount vegetarianism as merely a diet for radicals or fanatics are grossly misinformed. Vegetarianism is reinforced consistently by medical, scientific, ecological, and economic facts and surveys, and has been utilized by many cultures over thousands of years in many parts of the world.

The number one perpetrator of the "myth of vegetarianism" is, for obvious reasons, the meat industry in this country. Food is America's biggest business—$270 billion a year. Advertising on food amounts to $2.5 billion. The meat industry, therefore, constantly barrages the American public from birth to death with the illusion that meat is the most necessary ingredient in a healthy and enjoyable diet.

Baloney!

One of our biggest illusions in this society is that in order to "do a hard day's work" you've got to eat a hearty meat-and-potatoes diet. The *fact* is that a vegetarian diet of grains, complemented with vegetables and dairy products, can provide a 220-pound halfback or ditchdigger or carpenter with even more stamina than a T-bone and baked potato.

We cannot continue to consume meat in the gross quantities that we habitually do and live a truly healthy life. Never before in the history of man have a people had so much to eat. We overstuff ourselves with rich, highly indigestable foods and believe it's the right way to eat. We've taken our opulence for granted, as if this is the way things have always been. But man has never lived this high off the hog. And, frankly, it's killing us!

So You Want to Be a Fugitive?

You can make a change in spite of all those years of conditioning and centuries of tradition. You can get off the meat habit. But it ain't gonna be easy!

The first major obstacle you'll have to overcome is your family and friends. It starts with the looks they'll give you when they find out you don't eat meat anymore. They'll make you feel like a cross between Judas Iscariot and Bozo the Clown. They'll tell you that you won't get enough protein. They'll tell you you're gonna get sick. They'll even tell you you're gonna die!

Don't let any of this worry you. I have found that the people who are most strongly opposed to vegetarianism are those who are the most ignorant of the facts.

In order to stay a vegetarian, you'll need some strong reasoning on your side. You're going to need to be informed. I have always felt that the acceptance or rejection of vegetarianism should not be based on emotion, conditioning, prejudice, or nutritional gossip, but on a careful consideration of the facts. This book is meant to be the place where you can start to learn the basic facts about

Part Two

IF IT'S GOOD ENOUGH FOR PYTHAGORAS, IT'S GOOD ENOUGH FOR ME: A SHORT HISTORY OF VEGETARIANISM

vines. There are sweet-flavored herbs, and vegetables which can be cooked and softened over the fire, nor are you denied milk or thyme-scented honey. The earth affords a lavish supply of riches, of innocent foods, and offers you banquets that involve no bloodshed or slaughter; only beasts satisfy their hunger with flesh, and not even all of those because horses, cattle and sheep live on grass."

He was an eloquent rascal, wasn't he? He was also highly disciplined. The meals of Pythagoras are described by Diogenes as bread and honey in the morning and raw vegetables at night. He also felt such a deep kinship with his fellow animals that at sunset he'd stroll the beach and pay the fishermen to throw their catches back into the sea. Pythagoras also had a fondness for petting wild bears—a practice I suggest you avoid as vigorously as meat.

The Romans

The Greek tradition of vegetarianism survived in Roman culture. Although rich Romans gorged off meat nightly, there were a few who viewed this orgiastic behavior in a saner perspective. The famous Roman historian and biographer, Plutarch, was said to have given the following speech at a huge banquet.

Can you really ask what reason Pythagoras had for abstinence from flesh? For my part I rather wonder both by what accident and in what state of mind the first man did so, touched his mouth to gore and brought his lips to the flesh of a dead creature, he who set forth tables of dead, stale bodies and ventured to call food and nourishment the parts that had a little before bellowed and cried, moved and lived. How could eyes endure the slaughter when throats were slit and hides flayed and limbs torn from limb? How could his nose endure the stench? How was it that the pollution did not turn away his taste, which made contact with sores of others and sucked juices and serums from mortal wounds?

Cornaro describes himself between ages thirty-five and forty as being in constant pain from colic, gout, and a perpetual low-grade fever with accompanying thirst. "From these natural and acquired disorders the best delivery I had to hope for was death, to put an end to the pain and miseries of life."

In his despair, as a last resort, he decided to try a regimen of simple food and give up his habit of drinking three or four bottles of wine nightly. To his amazement, he enjoyed a renewed state of good health and after several more months was entirely cured.

After that, Cornaro not only permanently abstained from meat and alcohol but also avoided any other damaging influences such as extremes of cold, heat, and fatigue. In short, he followed the sober, quiet life, lived to be one hundred, and in the end became, as he described it, "my own physician."

Leonardo's vegetarianism came from the heart and Cornaro's out of physical necessity. Rousseau, the great philosopher of the Enlightenment, however, espoused vegetarianism, not surprisingly, for philosophical reasons. "It is nature which is already perfectly adapted to man's needs. Thus man should try to live within the natural order of things," he explained.

Vegetarianism, Rousseau rightly believed, followed this natural plan, and he concluded that meat-eaters were usually more violent and cruel than other men. Therefore, a vegetarian diet would result in a more compassionate person. From this Rousseau argued that butchers should not be allowed to testify in court or serve on a jury. I don't quite follow his logic, but who am I to argue with Rousseau?

As far as diet was concerned, Rousseau not only felt a vegetarian menu was in order, but that no butter or oils should be used for cooking and that no seasoning should be added until after the food was cooked. In those days such thinking was radical, indeed.

A contemporary of Rousseau, Ben Franklin, the inventor and statesman, was the first American vegetarian of note. At age sixteen, Franklin read Thomas Tryon's *The Way to Health, Long Life and Happiness,* a discourse on temperance, and immediately took up a meatless diet. Irascible, frugal, clean-living Ben, the man who gave us "a penny saved is a penny earned," embraced vegetarianism mostly because, as he so eloquently put it, "It saved me money."

Upon hearing those words, Leonardo would have stirred in his sarcophagus!

Other famous American vegetarians were Henry David Thoreau and Ralph Waldo Emerson. Among Nobel Prize winners, Albert Schweitzer and Albert Einstein did not eat meat.

Gandhi

Mohandas Karamchand "Mahatma" Gandhi not only practiced vegetarianism for its health and moral benefits, but used it as a political weapon as well. Never in history has one man rallied an entire people so forcefully around the ethics of a diet.

In India in the early twentieth century a philosophical issue was ripping apart the fabric of society. And meat-eating was at the center of it all. The English had conquered India and so dominated political and social life that many Indians, looking for a vital difference between the two cultures that would explain the English superiority, eventually blamed the Hindu tradition of vegetarianism. The English ate meat, and many young Indians thought it better to join them than to be beaten. However, so thoroughly was India steeped in Hindu tradition that when they tore at the roots of the religion, they tore at the roots of the nation.

Indian cultural pride degenerated because of a new-found taste for materialism. But Gandhi's charismatic power, his moral example, and his total rejection of mate-

rialism eventually pulled together the Indian people. His nonviolent philosophy, of which vegetarianism was at the heart, led to India's eventual freedom from British rule and to a renewed faith by the people in themselves and their nation.

"It is necessary to correct the error that vegetarianism has made us weak in mind, or passive or inert in action," said Gandhi. "I do not regard flesh food as necessary at any stage."

He eventually wrote five books on vegetarianism. In these books he tried to teach the Indian people that the blame for their malnutrition and poverty was due to a lack of education, not a lack of meat. And he tried to exemplify in his life and by his example that a simple meatless diet was healthful.

Gandhi's dietary habits were Spartan. He never touched food past sunset, and his entire food for the day consisted of eight tolas (about three ounces) of germinating wheat, eight tolas of sweet almonds made into paste

postwar England just finding such items was no piece of cake, so Shaw would send his cook out on forays in his chauffeur-driven Rolls Royce to hunt for the foodstuffs he enjoyed. Food became very important to him and his mealtimes were legendary. He was said to spend at least three hours over breakfast and another three hours over lunch. Dinner, however, was little more than a Shavian snack, taking him only an hour and a half to eat.

As Mrs. Laden, his cook, described it, "I rarely saw him (between meals, mind you) without a large chunk of cake heavily coated with sugar icing in his hand. One day, as he walked into the street to say goodbye to Greer Garson, who always came to see him when she was over from Hollywood, I saw him munching at the same time on an enormous piece of cake covered with marzipan and thick icing."

As you can see, Shaw had a sweet tooth—a prodigious one, in fact. At the traditional British teatime he eschewed tea for a large glass of milk to wash down the many chocolate biscuits and slices of fruitcake he enjoyed so much. Mrs. Laden often found him in the evenings seated with a bowl in his lap, stuffing sugar in his mouth by the spoonful. Sometimes it was a jar of honey instead.

Despite these indulgences, Shaw, who was well over six feet tall, always retained a slim and slender figure through vigorous exercise, including long walks around his estate. He weighed himself every morning to make sure he did not gain so much as an ounce from day to day, and demanded that Mrs. Laden write out scrupulously the calories in each dish she served him.

Archibald Henderson once asked him, "How do you succeed in remaining so youthful?"

"I don't," Shaw shot back. "I look my age. It is the other people who look older than they are. What can you expect from people who eat corpses?"

Shaw, who lived to be ninety-five, once described how he'd like his funeral to be conducted. "My hearse will be followed not by mourning coaches but by herds of oxen, swine, flocks of poultry and a small traveling aquarium of live fish, all wearing white scarves in honor of the man who perished rather than eat his fellow creatures."

Are You Turning Your Body into a Garbage Can?

The standard scene when I go out to eat with a group of nonvegetarians always goes something like this: We sit down, we order, and as soon as the waitress leaves they'll ask me "Why are you a vegetarian?"

I always answer, "Wait until after dinner because you won't want to hear what I've got to say before you eat."

Immediately they insist on an answer—"Don't worry! My stomach is made of cast iron."

So then I start to talk about the worms routinely found in meat, and the thirty-eight or more chemicals that the meat industry pumps into meat, and what a pig eats, and so on and on. By the time the meals show up, their appetites usually have disappeared.

Talking to people about vegetarianism is always a treat for me. One of my most memorable speaking engagements involved a group of high-powered executive types all staying at a $300-a-night resort in Hawaii. These were people who were all very successful—confident in their life-styles and directions. I knew most of them personally

That broke up the whole room. Everyone got a good belly laugh.

"Let me tell you why that pot of yours is the size it is. You go out to dinner and you have a few cocktails, and then you take your time over the entrees, and by the time you get that steak in your system it's nine or ten o'clock at night. Then you have a nightcap or two or three, and finally you plunk yourself down in bed. You're loaded down with alcohol and meat with your kidneys, liver, arteries, and heart begging for mercy.

"The next morning you're not feeling all that dandy, so what do you do? You start the day off with coffee. A lot of coffee! And what does coffee do? It gives you a fake hype. So now your taste buds are rolling and the cycle starts all over again. You're hooked. You're a slave to your taste buds."

I looked slowly around at this room full of successful people.

"You've all done a lot of intelligent things in your lives or you wouldn't be sitting here. But you don't give a damn about your body. Why? Why do people turn their bodies into garbage cans? Think about it. You buy a garbage can in a store and it's nice and shiny. Then, after a year or two, it's a mess, caked with crud and all banged up. That's exactly what people look like after they've abused themselves for years. Their bodies are absolutely ugly—big bulbous noses, veins popping out all over their faces, huge stomachs, and flab from chin to ankle. They have literally become garbage cans.

"And, you know, it's all because people base their lives on four inches. From the time you put the food to your lips until it hits your throat, the four inches it travels on your taste buds control your lives. After those four inches, there's no more feeling—no more gratification—and so no real reason why we should stuff ourselves with all that garbage.

"If people could put that four inches in perspective,

and diminish the importance of that sensual rush by realizing the long-term effect of what they're doing, we'd all be a lot healthier.

"Face it. There's only one real reason why people eat meat. Because it tastes good. Meat-eaters are like cigarette smokers. Cigarette smokers tell you they know they shouldn't smoke because it's bad for their lungs, their fingers are yellowed, their clothes smell, the curtains have to be cleaned constantly, there's the potential of heart disease or cancer, they're coughing up mucus . . . They know all the reasons why they shouldn't smoke—*but they gotta have it!*

"It's the same story with meat-eaters. Their reason for eating meat is simply that it tastes good. In a way, just like a cigarette smoker, a meat-eater is a drug addict. It's the chemicals that they pump into meat that they're addicted to.

"Why don't we give a damn about our bodies? If I asked you what was the most important thing to you—your job, your car, your house, or your life, what would you answer? Your life, of course. Then why do you pay incredible amounts of money to insulate your house, to own the right car, to make sure your house is secure from intruders, while not giving a damn about your body—the single most important element in your life. When your body goes, the rest goes with it. You may have alarms and locks all over your house, but you've invited the murderous thief right in the back door to take your life."

That little talk turned out to be one of my most rewarding experiences, because I still get letters from many of the people present that morning. I've received responses from nearly 100 of the people there who have since at least *reduced* their consumption of meat. Several are now vegetarians. Also, remember, many of them head their own companies and thus are in a position to influence many other people, so it's all been very satisfying.

I just wanted to let them know a little bit about their

41

istics in common that separate them from all other animals. For example, all carnivores have relatively uncomplicated digestive systems that measure about three times the length of their bodies. These are made for the fast digestion and elimination of rapidly decaying food—namely, flesh. Carnivores also have very acidic urine, and the digestive juices of their stomachs are high in hydrochloric acid which enables them to digest tough muscle tissues and even bones.

It's also been found that carnivores can handle almost unlimited amounts of fat and cholesterol, which means it's nearly impossible to find or produce arteriosclerosis in a dog. In experiments, up to half a pound of butterfat has been added to a dog's diet every day for up to two years with absolutely no change in serum cholesterol levels. The same amount of fat added to a man's diet (about 100 times normal levels) would cause great changes of the cholesterol in his blood and the fat buildup on his arterial walls.

Because they are mainly night hunters who sleep during the day when it's hot, carnivores don't sweat through their skin. Therefore, they don't need sweat glands and pores to regulate body heat by evaporation of water from the surface of the skin. When your dog gets hot, he sweats through his tongue and pants in order to cool off. Vegetarian animals such as the cow, the camel, and the deer spend lots of time in the sun and sweat like man does to regulate body temperature.

Now picture your dog eating. Another characteristic of carnivores is the way they "wolf down" their food. That is, they don't chew their food but rather tear it up and swallow it in chunks. Take one look at a man's mouth and it's obvious the opening is meant only for small pieces of food. Even then, he must chew these pieces into a fine mush mixed with digestive saliva before the whole mess will slide down his throat.

Probably the most significant and telling difference between the natural meat-eaters and the other mammals, however, is tooth structure. The carnivore's dental structure is made for eating raw flesh. Carnivores have powerful jaws and long, pointed canines that can easily pierce and tear flesh. Carnivores must kill with their teeth, which means cutting through tough hide, sinewy tendons, and bones. Also, carnivores do not have the massive molars that all vegetarian animals use for grinding coarse and bulky plant foods. A cat, for example, has almost no chewing capabilities at all.

Omnivores

The omnivores, such as the racoon and bear, are almost identical in anatomical structure and physiology to the carnivores. The only major difference is that the omnivores have a set of molars for chewing the plant foods that they eat.

Herbivores

The herbivores, including the elephant, the cow, the sheep, and the deer, generally live on grass and other plants which make their diet very coarse and bulky. The herbivores, therefore, have twenty-four grinding molar teeth, six on each side of the jaw, with eight cutting teeth on the bottom.

Herbivores don't chew their food simply by opening and closing their mouths like a dog or cat, but also use a slightly lateral motion which enables them to grind their food more effectively. Also, they have neither claws nor saberlike teeth, although some grass-eaters—like the rhinoceros, the bull, and the ram—have armor or horns for defense.

Herbivores have a complicated series of stomachs and a

45

long, convoluted intestine which is ten times the length of their bodies. Their saliva contains ptyalin, a substance used for the predigestion of starches, and both their saliva and urine are alkaline. Since herbivores, unlike carnivores, don't eat rapidly decaying flesh, digestion takes many hours.

Frugivores

The diet of the frugivores, such as the anthropoid apes (our immediate ancestors), consists largely of fruits and nuts. Their skin contains millions of pores and they have molars for grinding and chewing their food. Like the herbivores, the frugivores have alkaline urine and alkaline saliva with ptyalin. Their intestine is twelve times the length of their bodies, and is designed for slow digestion of fruits and vegetables. Also, the clawless hands of frugivores are designed for picking and eating their natural foods.

How About Man?

The inevitable question, of course, is, how does man stack up in comparison to these other mammals?

Well, man's digestive tract is twelve times the length of his body. His stomach and convoluted intestines are similar to those of the ape, but differ from the grass-eaters (who have two stomachs) and the flesh-eaters. Man has no hooves like the herbivores, or claws like the carnivores and omnivores. Instead, his hands are suited for the gathering and eating of fruits and vegetables, seeds and nuts.

Like the anthropoid ape, man has thirty-two teeth, including twelve molars and eight premolars for chewing plant foods, and a jaw that can move sideways for more efficient grinding of plant foods. Also, the popular notion that man possesses canine teeth is false. The misnamed "canines" that flank his four front teeth obviously have little in common with the long and pointed stabbing weapons found in the natural carnivores. Man also has alkaline saliva with ptyalin for the predigestion of starches.

All of this adds up to the fact that man never was, nor ever could be, a natural carnivore. Many experts seems to agree on that.

Baron Cuvier, the French naturalist, had this to say:

Fruits, roots, and the succulent parts of the vegetables appear to be the natural food of man; and his hands afford him a facility in gathering them; and his short and comparatively weak jaws, his short canine teeth not passing beyond the common line of the others, and the tuberculous teeth, would not permit him either to feed on herbage or devour flesh, unless those aliments were previously prepared by the culinary processes.

Carl von Linne (Linnaeus), who introduced binomial nomenclature, which named animals and plants *according to physiological structure,* said: "Man's structure, external and internal, compared with that of other animals, shows that fruit and succulent vegetables constitute his natural food."

William S. Collens and Gerald B. Dobkin added these thoughts:

Examination of the dental structure of modern man reveals that he possesses all of the features of a strictly herbivorous animal. While designed to subsist on vegetarian foods, he has perverted his dietary habits to accept food of the carnivore. It is postulated that man cannot handle carnivorous food like the carnivore. Herein may lie the basis for the high incidence of human arteriosclerotic disease.

47

So you can see that there's some pretty hefty evidence to support the opinion that, when you eat meat, you're stuffing yourself with a food your body just wasn't meant to swallow.

And that's the *good* news about meat.

Diseases and Impurities in the Animals We Eat

There are many things to consider when you sit down to a delicious steak dinner besides how good it tastes. For example, the diseases in the animal, the putrefaction of the meat caused by "curing," the waste products and other impurities that were in the animal at the moment it was slaughtered, the residues of pesticides it consumed in its lifetime, the phenomenon of "pain-poisoning," and the diseases that can be directly passed on to humans.

One of the basic facts that we almost always forget when eating the flesh of an animal is that, just like human beings, many of them become sick. If we eat a sick animal, we ingest what was in it at the time of its illness. For example, there are at least six hog diseases contractable by man—tuberculosis, undulant fever, influenza, swine erysipelas, listerellosis, and salmonellosis—and at least twenty-six we can pick up from poultry.

People who eat meat often just don't realize what they're getting into. If they could personally inspect the animals and see the quality of meat they were sometimes eating, they would be disgusted. People are continually

consuming meat that is infected with tuberculosis and cancer.

Farm animals contract an unusually high number of diseases because of overbreeding and overpopulation in the stress-filled environment of modern farming. Their vital organs degenerate rapidly due to overfeeding of excessive fats. They are castrated, which brings about glandular problems. Mastises, foot and mouth disease, fevers, tumors, and tuberculosis are common, and farmers frequently must have their livestock slaughtered rather than lose their valuable meat. In fact, cattle, sheep, and pigs with cancer are routinely used for meat. The tumors are simply cut away before the meat is allowed to pass inspection. And when cancer is detected in a chicken (and a recent government study showed that over 90 percent of the chickens in this country have leukosis, or chicken cancer) the tumors are cut away and the rest shows up in your local supermarket as chicken parts.

A 1972 statistical report of the U.S. Department of Agriculture lists the following diseases among animals whose carcasses were passed for food after removal of the diseased parts:

Epitheliomas (eye cancer) in cattle numbered 92,578. The eye and adjacent parts were removed; the remainder of the carcass was passed for food.

Abscesses or pyemia, meaning pus cells in the blood, in cattle numbered 439,837. The same disease in hogs, as one might expect, ran much higher—2,518,133. Among sheep and lambs there were 24,187 cases; in calves, 10,214. Liver abscesses in cattle ran to 3,596,302 cases, while the total of diseased cattle livers condemned was 6,057,920.

Pneumonia in cattle amounted to 144,210 cases; in sheep and lambs, 62,072; in calves, 23,242; in hogs, 161,544. All this in one year, and a marked increase over 1971.

This report continues for many pages and goes on to list more than fifty different diseases found in animals who were passed for consumption. If most of these diseases were discovered in a human, the poor guy would be hospitalized immediately. Animals suffering from the same diseases are sent to the butcher for your dining pleasure.

Undulant Fever

Brucellosis, also known as Bang's disease, Malta fever, and undulant fever, is one of the most common diseases transmitted from animals to man. It can cause headache, fatigue, chills, excessive sweating, and drastic weight loss. Since this bacteria can penetrate the skin, people contract the disease primarily through direct contact with infected cattle, pigs, or goats. Unless cured, it can become a chronic problem, disappearing for a time only to reappear again in unpredictable cycles, with symptoms that include arthritis, fever, stomach pains, and cardiovascular problems.

In 1947, there were 6,500 cases of undulant fever reported in the United States. The reported cases had dropped to a low of 190 in 1971. Unfortunately, however, the disease is difficult to diagnose and reported cases represent only a fraction of the total.

Trichinosis

It is probably impossible to find a parasite-free hog. Perhaps the most prevalent and damaging pest carried by swine is trichina—worms.

Humans get these worms by eating infested pork. The worms eventually travel through the bloodstream to every part of the body. They encyst themselves in the tissue after a few weeks and remain alive as long as you do. When these worms make their way to the eye and heart muscles, they can contribute to blindness and cardiac arrest.

A U.S. Department of Agriculture report in 1969 stated: "Today, based on the most recent incidence figures, between 80,000 and 90,000 trichina-infected hogs are marketed yearly."

The practice of feeding raw garbage to hogs may be the biggest problem, since untreated garbage is usually contaminated with trichina larvae. Unfortunately, only about 70 percent of the pork raised in this country is processed in plants that are under close inspection and, therefore, most of our pork probably carries live parasites. The chance of spotting infected meat is almost impossible since the cysts are nearly invisible to the naked eye.

The incidence of trichina in humans is as high as 95 percent in some populations of northern Canada, where the carriers are bears, walrus, and whales, and the disease is considered epidemic in Alaska. In a more suburban environment, the incidence of trichina infestation is nearly 12 percent in Washington. The United States has about three times as many cases as the world average.

A disease similar to trichinosis is toxoplasmosis. Though it usually does no serious harm to adults, it is extremely serious for babies. Toxoplasmosis causes more birth defects than rubella, muscular dystrophy, or congenital syphilis.

Like trichina, the toxoplasmosis parasite is usually contracted from undercooked meats like rare steaks.

Clinicians at Cornell University Medical College have estimated that there are 500 million to one billion human carriers of toxoplasmosis, and at least that many infected animals and birds. In the 1970s it was found that one-fourth of the population of Portland, Oregon, was infected with toxoplasmosis, while one-third of those examined in New Orleans had the disease.

Salmonellosis

The most common form of food poisoning is caused by salmonellosis. This viral disease finds its way into our bodies through meats and other products that come from infected animals, or from contamination by an infected animal or person.

Poultry is the biggest culprit.

Government inspectors have found salmonella contamination in over 50 percent of the poultry sold in supermarkets, and salmonella has been known to survive on the skin of frozen turkeys for more than a year. The National Communicable Disease Center estimates that 38 million Americans a year suffer from salmonella poisoning.

Outbreaks of salmonella poisoning often occur when a

large meal is prepared and the leftovers are not refrigerated immediately afterward. Chicken and turkey dressing are about the best breeding ground. Unless the bird is cooked long enough and to a high enough interior temperature, salmonella in the center of the stuffing will not be destroyed.

Symptoms of salmonella poisoning include headache, chills, cramps, and persistent diarrhea. The victim may also suffer from vomiting, fever, muscle weakness, faintness, and acute thirst.

One classic salmonella case happened in New Jersey in 1968 when a housewife prepared a traditional Thanksgiving dinner. She cooked a 23-pound turkey at 300 degrees for seven hours, and sixteen guests consumed the bird immediately afterward. All sixteen were in the hospital within seventeen hours. Three died, including the housewife and her son. The next day, after eating scraps from the table, the family dog died. All deaths were the result of salmonella poisoning.

Toxins in Fish

There are many naturally occurring toxins in fish that few people are aware of but many suffer from. Many finned fish and shellfish, for instance, produce naturally toxic substances that can cause anything from a simple allergic reaction to paralysis and death.

Tetradon poisoning can be contracted by eating a puffer fish. The symptoms include a tingling and numbness in the lips and tongue followed by a drunken uncoordinated feeling, followed by nausea, vomiting, convulsions, and paralysis.

You can get ciquatera poisoning by eating many types of fish, such as red snapper and barracuda that have ingested certain toxin-containing algae. This toxin is impervious to heat, so you can cook the fish into ash and you'll still be consuming the toxin. The symptoms include numbness and tingling of the lips and face, spreading eventually to the fingers and toes, followed by nausea, vomiting, and diarrhea.

Then there's a whole pack of marine invertebrates, such as *Gymnodinium brevis* (a protozoan responsible for producing "red tides") and *Gonyaulax catenella,* which are a favorite diet of mussels. If humans in turn eat the mussels, respiratory paralysis can occur within ten minutes.

When fish come in contact with the sewage of large cities, the runoff from industrial polluters, and the multitude of other contaminants we routinely pour into our waterways and seas, they become a source of disease.

No area is really safe, because fish that feed on coastal drainage may be caught where water is pure and fresh. Pesticide residues have been found in fish in areas as remote as Antarctica. Oil spills and radioactive waste material are also a constant danger, not only to the fish themselves (an estimated 15 million die annually from such pollutants) but to humans when they in turn consume these dangerous substances.

Substances such as mercury and arsenic accumulate in organisms that consume them. Thus, when a big fish eats a lot of little fish, the big fish retains the mercury and arsenic from all the little fellows. When we catch and eat the big fish these same poisons are passed along to us. "Biological magnification" is, in fact, a major threat in the use of all flesh foods, but it is most dangerous in fish.

Some deep-sea fish such as swordfish and tuna contain a quarter of a milligram of mercury for every pound of their body weight. It is estimated that as little as seventy milligrams of mercury can kill a human being. Since mercury constantly accumulates in humans (the mercury you ingest from a fish will be yours forever), it doesn't take a mathematical genius to realize that a steady diet of fish could kill you awfully fast. Symptoms of mercury poisoning include fatigue, headaches, tremors, and kidney damage, and it can also cause insanity and even death.

Chemicals We Pump into Our Animals

Eighty percent of the meat eaten in the United States comes from animals fed on medicated feed for all or part of their lives. Chemicals are added to meat to preserve it, to color it, to "texture" it, and to make it taste better. Arsenic is used as a growth promoter in chickens. Antibiotics are routinely administered to cattle to protect them against filthy stockyards (left filthy to save clean-up costs). And feed grain is so universally pre-doctored with antibiotics that, if a farmer wants it without additives, he must special-order it at a higher price.

In fact, there are 485 chemicals that can be added to food, none of which must be listed on any labels. Here's a list of just a few of the chemicals routinely found in meat:

Antibiotics like chlortetracycline, arsanilic acid, phenothiazine, phthalysulfacetamide, oxytetracycline, dimetridazole, ethylenediaminedihydriode, Terramycin, bacitracin, hygromycin B, neomycin, aureo 250, streptomycin, penicillin, chlortetra cycline, aureomycin, dihydrostreptomycin, and sulfonamides. Growth promoters and hormones such as diethylstilbestrol, melengestrol acetate, zeranol, arsenic, progesterone, testosterone propionate, furazolidone, tylosin phosphate, tri-p-anisolcholeroethylene, and dienestrol diacetate. The tranquilizers promazine, reserpine, and zinc bacitracin. And postmortem additives such as sodium nitrate, sodium nitrite, sodium sulphite, and sodium nicotinate.

To fully understand the extent that chemicals are used in the meat you eat, you've got to realize that the modern farm is not some bucolic pastoral retreat. It's a food production plant, plain and simple. All other considerations, including the health and comfort of the animals, are secondary to profit.

Years ago cattle roamed over green pastures, grazing on grass, drinking water, and resting when they felt like it. Things are very different now. Today cattle are fed hormones, antibiotics, insecticides, and tranquilizers. Many months before being slaughtered, steers are crowded into feed lots where they are again loaded up with hormones and tranquilizers, which causes them to more than double their weight in a few months of inactivity and gluttony. The life of a typical steer, once almost four years, is now only a year and a half.

A chicken's life is no paradise, either. Chickens today are raised in huge "factories" artificially lighted to keep them eating and egg-laying constantly. Over a quarter of a million hens a week are slaughtered in a typical farm. As many as 10 million chickens may be crammed into warehouses in which each bird lives in a space the size of a piece of typing paper. Because of growth hormones, antibiotics, and other "miracle drugs," a chicken that formerly took sixteen weeks and nearly ten to twelve pounds of feed to produce now takes eight to nine weeks and five pounds of feed.

Pesticides in Meat

Pesticide contamination of our meat is epidemic. As recently as 1965, the U.S.D.A. tested samples of poultry from every federally inspected plant in the United States for pesticide residues and found contaminated samples at every plant.

What makes pesticide contamination especially dangerous in meat is, once again, the phenomenon of "biological magnification." Livestock eat plants almost exclusively, and plants are at a very low level of the food chain. When we in turn eat these animals, we're eating at a higher level of the food chain. At each successive level, stored contaminants are passed along in ever-increasing concentrations to the next level. Thus, a "biological magnification" occurs.

To make matters worse, fat deposits in animals add an additional and even more striking magnification. Chemicals store up in fat deposits, so that an animal may carry dosages 100 times more concentrated than a single ingestion of the pesticide. The greater concentration is, of course, passed on undiluted to the customer—no extra charge! Meat can contain as much as fourteen times more pesticides than fruits, vegetables, and grains.

DDT is probably the most infamous of all pesticides. Even though its use has been banned, it will be with us for many years to come. Because of the insidious way in which DDT can be passed from one organism to another, no living creature on this earth is now safe from it. Penguins, elk, eagles, shellfish, and deer all have pesticide residues in their bodies.

Polychlorinated biphenyls, popularly known as PCBs, are a group of chemical compounds used widely by industry because of their resistance to heat. PCBs are found in snow and rain, which means they can, like a living entity, "migrate" thousands of miles. There is much evidence available to support the belief that PCBs can be found in every species of wildlife on this planet.

Worst of all, PCBs are even more dangerous than DDT, first because they are almost indestructible, and second, because they can remain in animal tissue much longer than DDT. The only way in which PCBs can be destroyed, in fact, is in a special incinerator at a temperature of 2,700 degrees F. PCBs have been known to cause miscarriages and stillbirths.

Antibiotics in Meat

At one time anthrax, blackleg, hog cholera, tuberculosis in cattle, diphtheria, and other diseases ran rampant in our livestock population. These diseases are now, of course, controlled by antibiotics administered by vaccination and also regularly mixed into feed. In fact, more antibiotics are now used by farmers than doctors—and on an uncontrolled basis because for animals no prescription is necessary. The farmer buys the drugs directly from a salesman and administers them as he sees fit!

Another reason that antibiotics are used in such abundance is because livestock are raised in such filthy conditions today that only antibiotics keep them from anemia, sickness, and death. In the environment of a factory-farm, where poor food, crowding, stress, and piled-up excrement are everyday facts of life, antibiotics are an absolute necessity. Why doesn't the farmer just keep things clean? you ask. The answer is that it's cheaper just to shoot his animals with antibiotics.

Fruits, vegetables, grains, and nuts don't contain antibiotics.

Growth Promoters

The female estrogen hormone diethylstilbestrol, or DES, was once the most widely used growth promoter by meat producers. It was banned as an additive in cattle feed in January, 1973. However, DES is still permitted in the form of pellets implanted in the ears of livestock, and is administered in this way to 75 percent of the cattle and sheep raised in the United States today. Cattle treated with DES produce meat with more protein and less fat, and gain up to 15 percent more weight than other livestock.

This "wonder drug," however, does have its drawbacks. It is known to cause vaginal cancer, breast cancer, and impotence. Also, many misuses of DES have been found. For example, farmers sometimes implant the DES pellet in a part of a chicken neck that is eventually consumed. Also, the sixty-hour estrogen-free waiting period required before slaughter of cattle is often ignored.

DES, however, may not be the most hazardous growth promoter in use today. The synthetic estrogen tri-p-anisolcholeroethylene is stored in human fat tissues and, therefore, is a more dangerous carcinogenic than DES because it stays in the body longer.

Another popular growth stimulant is arsenic, which is also the main ingredient in cattle and sheep "dip" used for the eradication of mites, ticks, and other parasites. The F.D.A. also allows arsenic in chicken feed, and chicken livers are known to contain high concentrations of this poison.

61

Tranquilizers

Tranquilizers are used by farmers for a variety of reasons. Besides calming the cattle in crowded, stressful, and filthy conditions, tranquilizers permit them to eat more food. Because their metabolisms are artificially reduced, they then gain weight at even more accelerated rates. So, if you feel a little lethargic after finishing a big T-bone, it may be more than satiation you're feeling.

What Slaughtering Can Do

You know how your blood rushes when you feel endangered? The same thing happens to an animal about to be slaughtered.

Just before and during the agony of being slaughtered, adrenaline is coursing in huge amounts through the animal. Adrenaline is a powerful stimulant that drastically raises blood pressure. When you eat an animal containing adrenalin, you receive a comparable dose.

Preslaughter stress, in fact, has been a major concern of the meat industry for some time because the meat actually changes color if an animal undergoes excess trauma. And excess trauma can understandably happen pretty frequently when someone is about to slit your throat or drive a stake through your head.

In addition to this so-called "pain-poisoning," there are many waste products left in an animal at the time of its slaughter. During life the body is washed by the blood which carries waste to the liver, kidneys, and skin for elimination. When the heart stops, the cleansing process stops, leaving in the carcasses toxic wastes such as urea and uric acid. Contrary to popular belief, these wastes are not eliminated when the dead animal is bled.

What the Butcher Does when He Gets His Chance

After the farmer is through adulterating the meat you eat, the butcher gets his turn. You might say at this point that your troubles have only just begun.

The process known as "curing" adds poison to your meal. When an animal dies, rigor mortis sets in and the meat toughens. Only putrefaction, or rotting, tenderizes it. The meat is then transported to the warehouse, on to the butcher shop and, finally, to the supermarket. There it's packaged and placed in meat racks, where it sits until you come along and buy it. You then lug it home, stick it in the refrigerator and, finally, cook and serve it. By this time, billions of pathogenic organisms producing highly toxic poisons have begun to breed on your innocent little burger.

But never fear, your butcher knows how to handle these problems. Sodium sulphite and sodium nicotinate, for example, can make an unappetizing piece of meat look like a fresh, blood-red sirloin steak. These chemicals are the real "miracle drugs" in a butcher's "doctoring" bag. Many chickens are also given their golden-yellow look by adding coloring to their feed, or by injecting them with the enzyme hyaluronidase. If you've ever purchased meat that looked delicious but tasted bad, it's very likely that it has been treated with these chemicals.

Sodium nitrite and sodium nitrate are used as preservatives to slow down putrefaction in cured meat and meat products, such as hotdogs, bacon, ham, luncheon meats, sausages, and poultry. Sodium nitrite used to be prescribed for high blood pressure and, in fact, your blood

63

pressure can be lowered by eating meats treated with nitrites—whether you need the treatment or not.

Under certain conditions, nitrites combine with amines found in meats and other foods, such as wine and beer, to form nitrosamines called by the F.D.A. "one of the most formidable and versatile groups of carcinogens yet discovered." In experiments, malignant tumors have been induced in every species of animal so far exposed to nitrosamines.

Diseases Related to Meat-Eating

After you've learned exactly what's in a piece of meat, I'm sure it won't surprise you that meat-eating is closely linked with the two major killers in our society—heart disease and cancer.

Americans today spend $140 billion annually on medical care, which is about $120 billion more than they spent in the 1950s. Meat consumption has similarly soared. In 1950, the average American ate 60 pounds of beef yearly. Today, he eats 125 pounds.

Heart Disease

The relationship of animal fats and heart disease is probably the strongest reason I can give you to lay off meat. Half of America's death toll comes from heart attacks and strokes.

One of the main forms of heart disease is arteriosclerosis—hardening of the arteries. The disease occurs when certain fatty substances coat the blood vessel's inner wall, blocking the flow of blood. When a blood clot cannot pass through the reduced diameter of the vessel, the heart itself is denied blood and the victim suffers a heart attack.

There are several factors that lead to arteriosclerosis, but the major cause is high cholesterol. A certain amount of cholesterol in the body is normal and healthy, but when it builds to the point where the vessels begin to clog, you're in trouble. There is no clear evidence to pinpoint exactly what causes this build-up of cholesterol, but present research strongly indicates that the food we eat is the major culprit. When you consume too much fat, whether of the saturated, unsaturated, or polyunsaturated varieties, your cholesterol level will rise. To keep serum cholesterol at a proper level, a person should get no more than about 15 percent of his or her calories from fats. Unfortunately, the average American on a meat-centered diet consumes 45 to 60 percent of his or her calories in fats.

Although hog meat, because of its high saturation of fat, contributes heavily to arteriosclerosis, beef is actually the biggest problem. The reason is that the beef eaten by Americans today is fattier and less nutritious than twenty-five years ago. Due to modern farming methods, steers are now artificially fattened through hormones, systematic overfeeding, and almost no exercise, so that almost one-third of their total weight becomes fat. Naturally raised, grass-fed beef is 5 to 10 percent fat.

One of the most striking examples of the difference between a low-fat and a high-fat diet was discovered during the Korean War. Americans killed in battle had advanced arteriosclerotic damage to their blood vessels and hearts even in their early twenties, whereas the Korean soldiers examined were almost free of blood-vessel disease. The Americans' diet, of course, was heavily weighted with meat, eggs, cheese, milk, and butter—42 percent of their diet, in fact, was fat. The Koreans, on the other hand, were basically vegetarian, with a diet containing less than 15 percent fat.

Further studies have shown that in countries where meat consumption is high, the mortality rate for heart disease is correspondingly high. In the U.S., Canada, and Australia, for example, heart disease is about ten times that of Japan, Italy, and Greece—the developed countries with the lowest meat consumption.

A study involving Japanese people in Japan, Hawaii, and the United States is also very revealing. Although all the people studied had similar hereditary backgrounds, they had different diets. The study showed that the closer a person adhered to the traditional Japanese ancestral diet (which contains less than 10 percent fat), the lower was the incidence of heart disease, no matter where the person lived. Of course, those Japanese living in the mainland United States tended to have a higher rate of heart disease than those living in Hawaii, and a much higher rate than those in Japan.

Cancer

When you barbecue a steak, the fat dripping into the fire can produce a byproduct called benzopyrene—one of the chief cancer-producing agents in tobacco smoke. The benzopyrene then goes up in the smoke from the burning charcoal and coats your steak. Thus a two-pound steak, well-done, can contain as much benzopyrene as 600 cigarettes. When mice were fed low doses of benzopyrene they developed bone cancer, stomach tumors, and leukemia. Methylcholanthrene, another chemical strongly linked to cancer, is also formed when the fat in meat is heated to a high temperature, whether the meat is barbecued, broiled, or fried.

Studies have also shown links between cancer of the

colon and meat-eating. The amount of time taken for the food of a heavy meat-eater to travel through the digestive tract is approximately five days, whereas, in a vegetarian, the process takes about one day. The longer putrified food is allowed to stay in the digestive tract, the greater is the irritation to its sensitive tissues. The incidence of colonic cancer is very high in the United States and other countries where a high-fat diet is prevalent, but not in Japan, India, and Africa, where the consumption of fat is significantly lower.

Kidney and Intestinal Diseases

There are over five million cases of acute intestinal illness in the United States every year. Many of these cases can be directly attributed to overconsumption of meat.

To put it simply, a meat diet creates more waste products for the kidneys to get rid of. Meat-eaters require at least three times more work from their kidneys to eliminate nitrogenous wastes than do vegetarians. While you're young, your kidneys can take this overload. As you age, the kidneys begin to break down from overwork. In America today, healthy kidneys in people over forty-five are the exception rather than the norm.

The Ethical Side of Vegetarianism

Vegetarianism is intrinsically linked with such ethical and moral considerations as the preservation of life, cruelty to animals (both through inhumane farming methods and barbaric scientific experimenting), and the ecological fact that we could eliminate starvation in the world by raising crops for human consumption rather than to feed the animals we eat.

Ecological Considerations

The population explosion and the world food shortage have had devastating effects. One and a half billion people are either hungry or malnourished, and nearly 500 million simply don't have enough food to survive. Every six seconds someone in the world starves to death—between 10,000 and 14,000 persons a day, and at least 3.5 million a year. One child dies every 56 seconds in Latin America alone!

The fact is that the world population many years ago grew beyond the point at which it could be supported by a meat-centered diet. There is a very simple solution to this global problem: Eliminate meat as the main source of food in the diet of the most wealthy countries.

In the United States we use five acres of agricultural land to feed a single person, compared to less than one-quarter of an acre in Japan. If we simply adjusted our diet and food production to match the Japanese diet more closely, we could feed 16 billion people adequately on what we now use to feed 1 billion.

Instead, meat consumption in the United States is increasing. In 1960, the average American ate 190 pounds of meat. Today, he eats 300 pounds. Some 45 percent of our arable land is, therefore, used to graze livestock. Only 17 percent is used for raising crops, and most of those crops are grown to feed livestock. And consider this: During the final four months of a steer's life, through overfeeding he gains 600 to 800 pounds. During this time he consumes over a ton of feed. Multiply that by the millions of steers all munching away at once, and you've got a situation in which livestock consume 97 percent of the nation's legumes, 90 percent of its grain, and 80 percent of its fish. These same animals supply us with only 20 percent of our food supply.

By using a little simple math it's not hard to figure that, if a significant amount of people gave up eating a significant amount of meat, we could feed a lot more people for a lot less money.

The Waste of Our Energy and Water

Our squandering of resources does not stop with our poor utilization of grain supplies. When you consider the irrigation of crops (remember, 90 percent of crops are fed to livestock), livestock drinking water, and the water used for meat food preparation, a meat diet requires eight times more water than a pure vegetarian diet. To put it into dollars and cents, it costs twenty-five times more to produce a pound of meat than a pound of vegetables. With ever-increasing demands on our water supply by a growing population, can we afford this waste?

Not only do meat producers use up a good deal of our water supplies, they pollute most of the rest of it. In fact, meat producers are the number one industrial polluters in our nation, contributing to more than half the water pollution in America. If you need firsthand proof, just drive by any stockyard. That overwhelming stench is created by waste matter that eventually percolates into the soil and then into the water table that feeds lakes, streams, and rivers.

The slaughterhouse produces its appalling stench with grease, carcass dressings, intestinal waste, and fecal matter, and all this is sent into our sewer system, ending up who knows where. These wastes can be several hundred times more concentrated than raw domestic sewage, containing tremendous amounts of fat, nitrates, and phosphates.

And that's not all we waste. It takes a farmer who is plowing and harvesting vegetable crops one calorie of fossil fuel energy to produce one calorie of food energy. But meat producers (who must transport food stuffs to their livestock and then transport the livestock to ranches, feedlots, slaughterhouses, and butchers) use about 100 times that amount of energy.

If the whole country went vegetarian tomorrow, we would use 40 percent less fuel overnight. That means we wouldn't need as much imported oil, and the price of gas would be back to 35 cents a gallon and ... Oh, well, at least it's a lovely dream.

The Cruelty of Modern Farming

The profit motive behind the factory farms of today that causes important environmental questions to be ignored also creates an atmosphere of systemized cruelty to animals. Modern farming is not the pursuit of gentle country folk. It is an assembly line run by big corporations. There is no place for gentility, or sentimentality, or for the idyllic environment most of us envision.

The modern farm is a competitive business that looks for any method available to increase production and cut costs. Animals are castrated, branded, overfed, denied exercise or sunlight, and transported long distances before they are slaughtered. A chicken averaging three and

72

a half pounds is given so small a space to live in that every one of its natural instincts is frustrated. It can't scratch the ground, or dust-bathe, or build a nest, or even stretch its wings. In an average year, 15 percent of the birds will die from stress due to overcrowding.

Pigs are similarly imprisoned. They are made to sleep, eat, and defecate in indoor pens so small they cannot turn around. They are confined in this manner so they cannot exercise, which enables them to put on weight faster, and, also, so that more animals can be kept in a smaller area.

Of all the inhumanities of mass production farming, the worst is surely the raising of baby calves for high-quality veal. Veal is the flesh of a baby calf not yet weaned from its mother and thus not yet eating grasses. Its meat is characteristically paler and more tender than normal beef and, therefore, highly prized.

Since a calf of this sort under normal conditions averages about ninety pounds, there was never much profit in raising veal. But now things are different. The calf is taken immediately from its mother at birth and tied up in a stall one and a half feet wide by four and a half feet long. This makes it impossible for the calf to exercise, which keeps its flesh tender and free from muscle. The calf is then fed a totally liquid diet of nonfat milk, plus growth-promoters, until it reaches a bloated weight of 350 to 400 pounds. Then it is led on wobbly, undeveloped legs directly to the slaughterhouse.

Experimenting with Animals

Perhaps the greatest cruelty that man inflicts on animals is his use of them for scientific research. The toll of maimed, abused, poisoned, and butchered animals for "the advancement of man" is staggering. A 1971 Rutgers University survey showed that the total animals used in

U.S. laboratories were 85,000 primates, 500,000 dogs, 20,000 cats, 700,000 rabbits, 46,000 pigs, 23,000 sheep, 1.7 million birds, 45 million rodents, 15 to 20 million frogs, and 200,000 turtles, snakes, and lizards. Or, in total, more than 63 million animals.

Many experiments are performed on animals that cause excruciating pain without any direct benefit for humans. Limbs are amputated, animals are injected with horrible diseases, including cancer, cooped up, tied up, and then, when they fail to survive, thrown on the dung heap.

The Slaughterhouse

It has been said that if we all had to kill our own meat, most of us would be vegetarians. We are conditioned by the meat industry to believe that the systematic slaughter of animals is somehow respectable; that these animals are willingly led to a quick and painless death, smiling all the way to the slaughterhouse. One visit to a slaughterhouse will rob you of that comforting illusion forever.

The day I visited a slaughterhouse, it was a sunny Tuesday morning in Los Angeles. The birds were tweeting and the morning air was fresh and I remember very well the pleasant drive to the downtown location of the "processing plant." I had been a vegetarian for a few months and a friend told me that a trip to the slaughterhouse was a must. So I went prepared for the worst. But it was worse than I would ever have imagined.

It's always the things that surprise you about an experience that stick in your mind most vividly. Oh, I thought I'd see slaughter and I wasn't disappointed—spikes were slammed through the skulls of sheep, the throats of baby calves were slit, pigs comings in one after another on a long conveyer belt were electrocuted with high-powered stun guns. But it was the *smell* of the place that hit me first and that really shocked me—a horrible, overwhelming stench that I recall as vividly today as at that moment. As soon as I stepped out of my car, the stench hit me—the smell of death, the foul odor of animals being opened up with all their cancerous organs and pus sacs and waste matter.

Then I saw the looks on the faces of the animals being led to their death. And I knew that those animals—whose sense of smell is far superior to ours, who live by what their instincts tell them—*knew* without doubt what was ahead of them. They could *smell* it.

And they could also hear it. The screeching and the screaming of the animals was so loud that, most of the time, I could not hear the man leading the tour.

I've always admired the peacefulness of the cow. Cows are harmless creatures, slow-moving, easy-tempered. But when they were being unloaded from the transport trucks at the slaughterhouse, they were just simply freaking out. Some of them were actually dropping dead from fright. You could see the terror in their eyes. They knew exactly what was coming. And I knew that if it were I going down that slaughterhouse row, I would be experiencing exactly the same feelings of terror.

Now, I'm no shrinking violet. I played hockey until half of my teeth were knocked down my throat. And I'm extremely competitive on a tennis court—I'll dive for any ball on any surface. But that experience at the slaughterhouse overwhelmed me. When I walked out of there, I knew I would never again harm an animal! I knew all the physiological, economic, and ecological arguments supporting vegetarianism, but it was that firsthand experience of man's cruelty to animals that laid the real groundwork for my commitment to vegetarianism.

I believe that if you walk into a slaughterhouse and if you have any feelings of compassion, just the tiniest feeling for another living being, you will realize immediately that society has gotten things just a little out of whack.

75

Part Four

Going Vegetarian
Phase One:
The Nutritional Concerns

An Adequate Diet
Without Meat

I don't want to give you the impression that going vegetarian is free of problems. For example, I knew this man in his sixties whose health had been failing him, so he decided to become a vegetarian. After six months of a solid regimen of good eating and exercise, he felt like a new man. In fact, he was such a ball of fire that he and his twenty-year-old secretary decided to get married.

When his doctor found out about the wedding, he called the old gentleman into his office and sat him down and told him, "You know, too much of a good thing can kill you."

The old man got a worried look on his face, then shrugged his shoulders and replied, "Well, if she dies, she dies."

Yes, there are always some problems whenever you radically change your life-style. For example, will your relatives and friends survive your newfound energy and your new way of looking at and going about your life? Because the way you eat inevitably influences the way you live.

Probably the key to making a smooth transition from

your flesh-eating days to your salad days is a smooth change in your own attitude.

I am always asked, "What can I eat if I don't eat meat?" You can tell what the questioner is thinking. He's picturing his old steak dinner and suddenly someone nicks the meat off the plate and all that's left is some old mashed potatoes and frozen spinach parboiled into oblivion.

Inevitably, when you introduce vegetarianism to people, they feel as though you're trying to take something away from them, and most of all an *enjoyment*. They *enjoy* eating meat. What they don't realize is that they're about to gain a whole new world in which their taste buds will be freed from drugged meat and the salt, fats, and garnishes that go with it. To them, vegetarianism is a prison. They are wrong.

All knowledge is a kind of freedom—a freedom to have and make choices. And that's both a blessing and a burden. Once you know what's in that piece of meat, you've got a very important decision to make. You can't kid yourself anymore. You can't hide behind the illusion that meat is good for you. Vegetarianism is not a prison or a limitation. I have the freedom to eat whatever I want— sausage loaded with nitrites, charbroiled burgers, heavily "marbled" steaks. I simply *choose* not to.

Making the Change Gradually

An easy way to avoid the trap of self-sacrifice, the feeling that you're depriving yourself of something, is to make the change into vegetarianism gradually. That's probably the surest way to reach your goal of not eating flesh foods, and it's also usually the safest.

First, give up beef, veal, lamb, and pork; then chicken and turkey; and, finally, fish. At each step along the way you should be introducing into your diet more dairy products, beans, vegetables, and grains.

This gradual reduction of meat can help you avoid some of the temporary gastrointestinal disturbances caused by poor digestion of all the extra roughage you've suddenly introduced into your system. Since wholesome, fresh vegetarian foods are loaded with fiber, it's also advisable to learn to chew your food more thoroughly— good advice even if you don't become a vegetarian.

A second benefit from a gradual easing into your new vegetarian diet is the avoidance of the serious letdown that can accompany the change.

A person on a heavy meat diet is accustomed to the highly stimulating effects of the drugs in meats. When you take away the stimulant, you take away the effect. The resulting letdown is often attributed to low energy from a lack of protein in a vegetarian diet. However, since carbohydrates are the primary source of our energy, and a well-planned vegetarian diet usually means you're eating more carbohydrates than on a meat diet, this feeling is *not* related to protein deprivation. Plain and simple, it's a withdrawal symptom.

Of course, I went off meat cold turkey, so I'm not totally against sudden withdrawal. But to achieve this you have to know what kind of person you are. If you are strong and disciplined enough to give up meat immediately, do it. But if you want to reduce your consumption of meat slowly, then go about it that way. Remember the important thing is the result: Are you living a healthier life?

Another piece of advice that goes hand in hand with the gradual approach is: Don't be a zealot. I think Gandhi put it best. "What I want to bring to your attention," he said, "is that vegetarians need to be tolerant if they want to convert others to vegetarianism. Adopt a little humility."

In other words, after you've given up meat for a week, don't run through the streets banging a tin lid proclaiming you're saved. Don't stuff it down your family's or friends' throats. We all have a tendency to shout out loud when we think we've found something unique. Restrain yourself. It will save you a lot of unnecessary stress and, also, if you want others—especially those you love—to share what you've discovered, the best advertisement is your own healthy appearance and vitality. Oh, sure, by all means make the information available to them—let them know what you're up to. But let the sparkle in your eyes and your healthy skin and shiny hair do most of the talking for you.

By the same token, don't be hard on yourself if you backslide. Many people give up vegetarianism completely because they eat meat once or twice in a moment of weakness. If you do happen to go off your meatless diet, don't panic. You can always start it again. Vegetarianism is a habit that eventually turns into a life-style and then into a way of life. Remember, you are a vegetarian *every time you have a meatless meal.*

Is a Vegetarian Diet Adequate?

There seems to be one almost universal major fear of people considering a meatless diet. Is a vegetarian diet adequate?

Vegetarianism is often associated with faddism but let me assure you, it is not faddish, cranky, or weird. Evidence to the adequacy of a well-balanced vegetarian diet is beyond dispute. Throughout the ages, vegetarians have enjoyed greater longevity, endurance, and mental health.

In many parts of the world there are vegetarian cultures whose members are healthier than the meat-eaters living in the same area. Strict Hindus have adhered to vegetarianism since well before the birth of Christ. The tribes living in the Vilcabamba Valley of Ecuador eat less than an ounce of meat per week, and yet scientists have found that a significant percentage of the population lives beyond 100 years of age. A study of the men in Hungary who were 100 years or older found that they were almost all vegetarians.

One of the most celebrated of vegetarian societies, the Hunzas of the mountainous regions of northwest Pakistan, live on the simplest diet of wheat, corn, potatoes, onions, and fruits. They are renowned for their incredible endurance. They eat meat only once or twice a year. In 1964, Dr. Paul Dudley White, a noted American heart specialist, studied twenty-five Hunza men ranging in age from ninety to one hundred and ten years and found, even at that age, that they possessed normal blood pressure, blood cholesterol, and electrocardiographic patterns.

Probably the most conclusive studies done on vegetarians involved the Danish population during World War I.

The Allied blockade caused a critical shortage of food-stuffs in Denmark. The Danish government, therefore, sought the advice of Denmark's vegetarian society and of Dr. Mikkel Hindehede of the Laboratory for Nutrition Research in Copenhagen. The Danish population under his advice went almost entirely vegetarian. Their diet consisted almost exclusively of bran, bread, barley, porridge, potatoes, greens, milk, and a little butter. By using the grain formerly used to raise livestock, the Danish people were able to feed themselves and survive the war.

And they survived it with improved health and a significantly lower mortality rate—34 percent lower from non-infectious diseases. When the Danes went back to their regular diet after the blockade was lifted, the mortality rate immediately shot back up to what it was before the war.

A similar thing occurred in Norway during World War II when the Nazis occupied the country. The Norwegians ate more cereals, potatoes, vegetables, and skimmed milk and less meats, eggs, and cream. Deaths from circulatory diseases dropped 21 percent from 1940 to 1945. After the war the death rate returned to prewar levels.

Variety and Balance: The Keys to a Healthy Diet

The one principle that I emphasize to all new vegetarians is that they eat a varied and balanced diet. That's the key to a sane, healthy, and enjoyable approach to vegetarianism. Choose a wide selection of foods from the four basic food groups listed below. Never get into the rut of eating the same thing day in and out.

Also avoid the trap of trying to meticulously plot out your nutritional needs down to the exact milligram. Calculating exactly how many calories of this protein food and that mineral source they should eat often makes people into the kind of cranks who buy every vitamin supplement on the shelf to ensure they've got every possible nutritional angle covered. Be sensible. Would we all still be around if we didn't have within our means a way to get the nourishment we need without blowing the gross national product on vitamin pills? The best way to guarantee you'll get all those trace minerals and oddball vitamins, and all the other nutrients that make up a sound diet, is simply to eat a wide range of different foods.

And another thing: Eat *whole* foods. Stay away from the highly processed foods in packages, cans, and in frozen-food freezers. Our basic nutritional requirements are water, carbohydrates, protein, vitamins, minerals, and some fats. Whole foods often supply the entire range of our needs, whereas highly processed or refined foods often supply only one or two of these requirements.

The Four Basic Food Groups

1. Grains, legumes, nuts, and seeds:
   Grains: Some examples are rice, bread, oats, pasta, cereal, wheat germ, and flour.
   Legumes: Some examples are chick peas (garbanzo beans), pinto beans, kidney beans, peanuts, lentils, soybeans, and split peas.
   Nuts and seeds: Some examples are almonds, cashews, pecans, pistachios, pumpkin seeds, sesame seeds, sunflower seeds, and walnuts.
2. Vegetables: Fresh, wholesome vegetables of all varieties.
3. Fruits: Fresh fruits and fruit juices of all types.
4. Dairy products: Some examples are milk, cheese, yogurt, cottage cheese, ricotta, kefir, sour cream, and cream.

Protein

Protein! Protein! Protein! That's all you hear about these days. Am I getting enough protein? Well, if you're the average American, you're probably getting at least three times the protein you need, and about seventy times more protein than the average Asian consumes! And if you're a protein faddist who consumes protein-saturated drinks one, two, or three times a day, you're probably drowning yourself in the stuff.

Excess protein poisons your system by dumping into it too much uric acid, waste nitrogen, and other toxic substances that overwork your kidneys and liver. Protein has also been found to drastically stimulate aging, which explains why the Masai, an African tribe whose diet is almost exclusively meat, become old in their twenties. Other heavy meat-eating societies, like the Eskimos, the Greenlanders, the Laplanders, and the Russian Kirghiz, also have a shortened life expectancy of about thirty to forty years.

All nutrients are only safe or useful to the body up to a limit. In other words, because of our fears and lack of knowledge we are destroying our bodies by giving them nutrients well beyond their needs.

But don't misunderstand me—protein is vitally important to your body. Protein is a part of every living cell and is found in every organism, from an amoeba to a whale. In fact, only water is more plentiful than protein in the body. We are 20 percent protein by weight.

Only protein contains nitrogen, sulfur, and phosphorus—substances essential to life. Muscles, bones, and skin are made mostly of protein. And proteins are used to replace tissues that are continually breaking down and growing, like hair and nails. Protein is also crucial during periods of growth like childhood and pregnancy.

Protein is also essential in major metabolic functions, such as heat regulation and water balance. The bloated stomach commonly seen on starving children, for example, is caused by fluid allowed to accumulate in the interstitial spaces between the cells and is a direct result of protein deficiency. A lack of protein in the system can also cause mental and physical retardation, anemia, weight loss, irritability, and reduced natural immunities.

Getting the Right Amounts of Protein

As protein from your diet is digested, it breaks down into the organic acids called amino acids. Though it takes from a couple of days to seven years to deplete the body's reserves of other required nutrients, amino acid reserves are depleted in a few hours. Since cells must constantly be repaired and replaced (red blood cells have a life span of only about 120 days and the lining of the small intestine is renewed every day or two), it is pretty obvious that an adequate supply of protein must be maintained.

So *how much* protein do we need? Technically speaking, we need enough to keep our bodies in a "positive nitrogen balance," which means that there is more protein in the body than is being used. Since protein is made up mostly of nitrogen, if you measure the amount of nitrogen going in and out of the body you can figure your nitrogen balance. If you are in a negative nitrogen balance, then you are losing proteins from your muscles and you've got a problem.

Just as serious a problem is an excess "positive nitrogen balance." If you get more than about 16 percent protein in your diet, you'll have a negative mineral balance. The reason is that high amounts of protein set up an acid condition, and only calcium leached from the bones can neutralize this effect. The problem of brittle bones in old people is often attributed to a lack of milk in their diets. The fact is that their protein-saturated diets throughout their lives leach calcium (and many other important minerals such as zinc, iron, and magnesium) from their systems.

Mostly due to protein propaganda, in America today the average person consumes at least 20 percent of his or her diet in proteins, yet studies have shown that adults eating simply white rice as their main protein source maintained a positive nitrogen balance. This rice-centered diet was only 6 percent protein. I don't recommend eating only white rice, or even keeping your protein intake at 6 percent. A sensible level supported by the World Health Organization is between 10 and 15 percent.

If you know how many calories you should consume daily to maintain a sensible weight for your height and age and activity level, it is quite easy to compute your protein needs. Simply multiply your calorie intake by 10 percent for your minimum protein requirement.

There are several factors, however, that do vary protein requirements. There is evidence that stress in varying amounts causes protein deficiency. Fear or prolonged anxiety increases the levels of adrenaline in the system, which burns up protein. Loss of sleep, jet lag, fever, infection, surgery, and any other occurrences that upset normal metabolic patterns can also deplete protein supplies up to one-third over the normal rate. Pregnancy, infancy, and any period of rapid growth also increases protein need. But don't go overboard. If you're taking in over 15 percent of your calories in protein on a regular basis, you're doing yourself more harm than good.

But Does a Vegetarian Diet Supply Enough Protein?

If you ask a group of new or prospective vegetarians what their greatest fear is, they will almost universally answer, "Protein!"

The simple truth is that it's almost impossible *not* to get enough protein to meet your daily needs on a vegetarian diet, provided you eat wholesome and fresh foods from a variety of vegetarian food groups.

Dr. Fred Stare of Harvard University, and Dr. Mervyn Hardinge of Loma Linda University, conducted a study of 112 vegetarian and 88 nonvegetarian adult men and women, pregnant women, and adolescent boys and girls. The two doctors fed one group a diet containing 50 grams of protein daily, of which only 5 grams were animal (milk) protein; the second group ate 100 grams of protein, of which 60 grams were from animal sources. A third group was fed a high-protein diet of 160 grams, nearly all of it from animal sources. After two months the results showed that there were no significant nutritional or physical differences between the vegetarians. All groups exceeded twice their minimum daily requirements of protein.

The report further stated: "No members of the low-protein group, not even the hardest worker, who averaged about 5,000 calories' expenditure on a working day, suffered measurable deterioration in physical vigor ... it seems reasonable to conclude from this experiment that a daily protein intake of 50 grams, of which as little as 5 grams consists of animal protein, is perfectly adequate for good health and efficiency, providing, and this is a most important proviso, the diet is adequate in other respects, particularly calories."

We're all pretty familiar with the animal-derived protein sources such as meat, fish, eggs, milk, and cheese. But the fact is that most of the people in the world get their protein from nonanimal sources: grains (almost half of the protein consumed in the world is derived from grains), legumes, nuts, seeds, and vegetables.

Thus, even vegans, who get the bulk of their calories from vegetables, grains, and beans, will have little problem reaching their minimum protein requirements. And lacto-vegetarians who eat dairy products will, of course, have even less problem getting adequate protein. The fact is that if you eat a cup of oatmeal, two slices of toast, a peanut-butter sandwich, a cup of beans, a cup of rice, an ounce of mixed nuts, and two glasses of soy milk—you will get 58 grams of protein.

The table below shows the high-protein concentration of vegetarian foods as compared to meat.

PROTEIN SOURCE	GRAMS OF PROTEIN PER 4 OZ. SERVING
Hamburger	27
Porterhouse steak	22
2 eggs	12
Cashew nuts	20
Soybean flour	41
Ham	23
Flounder	18
Swiss cheese	32

PROTEIN SOURCE	GRAMS OF PROTEIN PER 4 OZ. SERVING
Cheddar cheese	32
Peanuts	28
Lentils	28
Cornmeal	11
Rice	7
Wheat flour	15.6

Protein Complementing—Yes or No?

Diet for a Small Planet, by Frances Moore Lappe, is a detailed volume of vegetarian nutrition and ecology that is, perhaps, the most influential book on the subject in the last twenty years. You can rarely open another volume on vegetarianism written since Lappe's book was published and not see her influence. Her research on a subject known as "protein complementing" is particularly influential. "Protein complementing" is the combining together of two "inferior" protein sources at the same meal in order to make up a "superior" protein, that is, one that contains all eight essential amino acids.

The body requires fourteen different amino acids, of which eight the body itself cannot manufacture and thus must get from the diet. According to Lappe, since the body cannot store amino acids, all of the essential amino acids must be present at the same meal. At the top of Lappe's list of high-quality protein foods are eggs and milk, because they contain all eight amino acids in sufficient quantity and in just the right combinations to adequately supply the body's need for protein. The protein in wheat, corn, rice, beans, nuts, and other plant foods is of lower quality, because in each of them one or more of the essential amino acids is present in such inadequate amounts that the entire protein value is diminished. According to Lappe, food-combining can elevate a protein source, inadequate in isolation, to a complete state. So the best way to get the most efficient use of protein is to eat a combination of protein foods (both complete and incomplete) at each meal. For example, peanut butter and bread, cereal and milk, and beans and rice are all protein combinations eaten instinctively by cultures throughout the world.

What does this all mean to you as a vegetarian? Well, according to Lappe, you can get a satisfactory combination of amino acids from a diet of grains, nuts, legumes, and vegetables, but you have to follow a complicated system of protein complementing that Lappe details in the final 300 pages of her book.

Many opponents of protein complementing have come forward in the last few years, none more well-spoken or outspoken than Nathan Pritikin, the author of *The Pritikin Program for Diet and Exercise.* In an interview with *Vegetarian Times,* Pritikin had this to say about protein complementing.

"It's completely wrong. The authors don't understand nutrition. The idea of balancing foods doesn't make any sense. Unfortunately, the book is one of the most misleading documents in the last few years because everybody now thinks food balancing is essential. They give the impression that vegetable proteins don't have sufficient percentages of amino acids."

The fact is that 80 percent of the protein we eat is broken down and reconverted into the fourteen nonessential amino acids that make up our muscle tissue. The body makes up a balance of amino acids from a pool of amino acids in the digestive tract. So you need only a general variety of food from day to day—not an exact balance of amino acids at every meal, as Lappe states.

Mrs. Lappe, in fact, later corrected her statements on the eight essential amino acids in a revised edition of her book when she wrote, "We are probably better able to utilize deficient amino acids than previously thought, since mechanisms may operate in the gut to redress the natural imbalance of amino acids in foodstuffs."

Another of Lappe's ideas that Pritikin strongly opposes is the notion that eggs are the ideal protein food. "We don't know the ideal," he says. "Nobody's experimented in that direction. But if, for example, you take the egg and feed it to humans as their principle source of protein, you require nine percent of total calories in protein to break even in nitrogen balance.

"However, if you take egg and potatoes, half and half, you now get by with six percent total calories in protein. You need fifty percent less protein than with egg alone. The body becomes much more efficient when you introduce vegetable protein. The book starts with one wrong premise and everything follows."

The point is well made. If you meet your calorie needs with a variety of wholesome, fresh food, you should be getting all the protein you'll require.

Fats and Cholesterol

Fat is just as important to your diet as protein. Fat is used for energy reserves so that your protein supply will not be used as fuel. Fat pads the internal organs from injury and is vital in both the production of body heat and as an insulator to preserve that heat. It is also required for the absorption of the fat-soluble vitamins A, D, E, and K.

On the other hand, too much fat can kill you. In the high fat concentration of a meat-centered diet, hormone and carcinogen levels are 1,000 times greater than normal. Excess fatty deposits significantly impair the cleansing action of the liver and kidneys and raise cholesterol to dangerous levels. Most important of all, excessive fat in the diet is closely associated with heart disease. The American Heart Association specifically recommends limiting the cholesterol in your diet as a means of reducing the risk of heart disease.

Saturated or Unsaturated—Does it Matter?

There is one very misleading direction in cholesterol maintenance—the importance of polyunsaturated fats.

Dietary fats are divided into two major groups depending on how many hydrogen atoms are capable of being bonded to their carbon chains. If fats are saturated with all the hydrogen they can hold, they are called saturated fats. If they are unsaturated because their double bonds remain available for more hydrogen, they are usually termed polyunsaturated.

In general, saturated fats, such as butter and lard, are solid at room temperature while unsaturated fats, such as most vegetable oils, are liquid at room temperature. Basically, then, animal fats are highly saturated, and vegetable and fish oils are highly unsaturated (except for coconut, palm, and olive oil).

The food manufacturers, in an effort to fatten profits, have spread the rumor that polyunsaturated fats are a panacea for coronary heart disease. This is simply not true. Although polyunsaturated fats are more easily digestible, some studies have shown that a diet loaded with polyunsaturates causes hair loss, diarrhea, and liver disfunction. Polyunsaturates also cause a blood condition known as "sludging." This reduces the blood flow, especially in the lungs, and, therefore, is most dangerous for people with diseases such as emphysema and asthma and for those who live in areas of highly polluted air.

While it is true that polyunsaturates contain no cholesterol, it is *fat,* as well as cholesterol, that affects the serum cholesterol—the cholesterol in the blood.

About 40 to 45 percent of the average American's caloric intake is fats—over 100 pounds per year for every adult. This amount is way over recommended limits or nutritional requirements. Actually, a well-balanced diet will contain no more than about 15 percent of its calories in fats of all types.

Carbohydrates and Sugar

Carbohydrates are usually divided into starches and sugars. They are made up of carbon, oxygen, and hyrogen, and are found in fruits, vegetables, grains, nuts, seeds, and the roots and cellulose of plants.

Carbohydrates are the body's main fuel for exercise, and they are much more efficient than fats or proteins as muscular fuel. An abundant supply of carbohydrates saves the proteins in your system for their job of body and cell maintenance.

Carbohydrates must first be converted into glucose before they can be utilized by your body. Glucose is one of the simple sugars and transports its fuels through the bloodstream. Starches are made up of complex chains of glucose and are, therefore, easily broken down in the digestive processes to form glucose for energy.

On the other hand, the carbohydrates in sugar and bleached and processed flours are empty of nutrients. Although these foods satisfy your appetite, they crowd out any other foods that could supply vitamins and minerals. Whole grains and legumes, however, supply the B-vitamins that the body needs to burn glucose as fuel, but, even more importantly, the proteins, fats, and roughage found in the complex carbohydrates slow down the digestion of the glucose and allow the sugars to burn up slowly and steadily. That's the reason why, when you eat a plate of spaghetti, for example, you don't feel the sudden rush and then let down you feel when you eat a chocolate bar, or doughnuts and coffee.

Carbohydrates from unprocessed whole grains and legumes can satisfy both your appetite and your nutritional needs. That's why I stress that a great proportion of your diet should consist of the complex carbohydrates.

Are Carbohydrates Fattening?

The popular notion that you should stay away from carbohydrates because they're fattening is a myth. Complex carbohydrates such as whole-grain breads, cereals, and legumes should become the staples of your vegetarian diet. They are fattening only when you're eating too many total calories. Otherwise, they are no more fattening than an equivalent number of calories of fat or protein.

The real culprits in the carbohydrate family are those that are highly refined—empty calorie foods like sugar, white flour, and alcohol. These processed carbohydrates fill you up with calories but have almost no nutrients. Also, because they burn up so quickly, they cause drastic and rapid fluctuations in your blood-sugar level.

The emphasis on processed carbohydrates in this country has caused a shift in our diets from mostly starch to mostly sugar. Seventy-five years ago, 55 percent of our carbohydrate intake was starch. Today, starch accounts for 37 percent. Sugars now occupy nearly 40 percent of our carbohydrate consumption—twice the amount we ate in 1920. Today, the average American consumes 2 pounds of sugar a week, 125 pounds a year (150 pounds a year for children) from hundreds of sources—table sugar, soft drinks, desserts, breads, sauces, and canned goods.

This emphasis on sugar has created massive physiological problems, including increased blood pressure, hypoglycemia, diabetes, embolism, and heart disease. Cirrhosis of the liver has been found in teenagers who drink too many soft drinks.

The best strategy is to stay away from refined sugar—even brown and raw sugar—and any processed foods that contain it. They are all basically sucrose, which lowers the blood sugar and triggers excessive insulin reactions. Also, honey, though superior to any other sweetener, is still a sugar and, like all sugars, fosters dental cavities, obesity, and emotional and physical ups and downs.

Fiber

Avoiding refined carbohydrates because they're low in fiber also does wonders for your elimination. The indigestible parts of the plant known as roughage or fiber, though they add nothing of nutritive value to your diet, can eliminate constipation and many accompanying ills.

The fiber in your food helps push the waste products through your system more rapidly, whch means these bacteria-laden substances have less time to putrefy in your system. Putrefaction of waste matter is considered by many experts to be a major contributor to illness— lowering the effectiveness of your body's immune system and fostering disease. Studies have shown that people who consume small amounts of fiber suffer high rates of cancer of the colon.

The best sources of fiber are whole-grain cereals, nuts, fruits, and vegetables. Vegetarians, by the way, consume large amounts of fiber (as much as 100 percent more than meat-eaters), so they don't normally need to concern themselves with adding more to their diets.

The Special Problems of a Vegetarian Diet

Veganism

Veganism is the purest form of vegetarianism. A vegan will eat no foods of animal origin, including eggs, milk, cheese, and yogurt. Many vegetarians eventually become pure vegans because they realize they can eat a nutritious, varied diet without consuming eggs or milk. Veganism is the most respected diet among vegetarians because it totally eliminates exploitation of animals. But veganism is a diet with serious limitations which must be understood fully before it is undertaken.

GETTING ENOUGH PROTEIN ON A VEGAN DIET

The most important questions that confront a vegan are how to get enough protein without eating dairy products, how to get enough vitamin B-12 (the only vitamin that cannot be supplied by purely vegetable sources), and how to eat a well-balanced diet.

In order to make sure that they get enough protein in their diets, vegans must get about 60 percent of their protein from grains, 35 percent from legumes, and 5 percent from leafy green vegetables. In order to know whether the 60 percent of your diet that is grain will meet your protein requirements, it's necessary to know which grains are highest in protein. For example, rice and corn are approximately 8 percent protein, while whole wheat is about 14 percent. Put simply, 2½ cups of a mixed variety of grains—rice, millet, bulgur and so on—and four slices of whole-wheat bread will supply the grain protein needs of the average adult male. The legume protein requirement (35 percent of the diet) can be met by eating one cup of cooked beans.

If you are getting enough calories from the four vegan food groups to maintain your weight, it's very difficult not to consume your protein needs for the day. Remember, fats from animal sources make up over 40 percent of the average American diet. Grains should replace these calories in a vegan's diet.

The best sources of protein for a vegan are almonds, Brazil nuts, cashews, pecans, and walnuts; sunflower and sesame seeds; beans, lentils, peas, peanuts, and soybeans; buckwheat, barley, whole oats, rice, whole rye, whole wheat, and wheat germ; and vegetables like potatoes and spinach.

GETTING VITAMIN B-12 ON A VEGAN DIET

Getting enough vitamin B-12 is perhaps the most crucial problem of a vegan diet. B-12, also known as cyanocobalamin, is present in meat, eggs, and milk but is not found in a readily assimilable form in vegetables. This is largely due to the fact that it is the only vitamin exclusively synthesized by bacteria. Therefore, because they can't manufacture it themselves, all animals get their B-12 from bacterial synthesis.

B-12 is stored in the liver and kidneys and is released whenever needed to other tissues of the body, but especially bone marrow. B-12 is important in cell metabolism and DNA synthesis and stimulates the formation of blood cells.

Lack of B-12 may lead to female infertility, pernicious anemia, fatigue, breathlessness, and indigestion. Among these symptoms, the nervous disorders are the most serious. Early symptoms include a tingling sensation in the feet and hands followed by a loss of feeling. This can eventually lead to "subacute combined degeneration of the spinal cord," which causes permanent injury and even death if B-12 is not taken to halt and reverse the degeneration.

There have been a few cases in which vegans have lived twenty years or more in good health without taking B-12 supplements, but that's a risky strategy for a vegan. The misleading thing about a B-12 deficiency is that the body has a store of the vitamin that can last at least five years, so that symptoms of a lack will not appear until a person has been a vegan for quite a while. It's then difficult to diagnose the problem, since no change in diet or life-style will have occurred in the recent past. Many times a B-12 deficiency is thought to be some other disease with similar symptoms, often wasting valuable time in correcting the problem.

However, there are many ways a vegan can get enough vitamin B-12 without resorting to foods, supplements, or pills from animal sources. (Lacto and lacto-ovo vegetarians, of course, have no problem getting full daily requirements of B-12, since eggs and milk are two of the richest sources of this vitamin.)

An excellent and delicious way to get a daily supply of B-12 is to drink fortified soy milk—which, incidentally, is one of the highest sources of protein available. There are a couple of things to watch out for, however. Most of the commercially produced soy milk is marketed for children who have a lactose intolerance and must get their milk from a nondairy source. Like so many of the foods produced for children in our society, soy milk is often heavily sugared and/or underfortified. Check the label for sugar and B-12 content. Or, better yet, learn to make your own soy milk.

Seaweed is also a good source of B-12 and a couple ounces a day will do the trick. Alternatively, you can take supplemental tablets, but this is a little tricky since most of the B-12 supplements are derived from animal sources. B-12, however, may also be produced by a fermentation of bacteria grown on vegetable matter similar to baker's yeast. So check the labels.

One other note of interest is a recently published study suggesting that large doses of vitamin C, used today to "cure" everything from a cold to cancer, may destroy most of your body's supply of vitamin B-12. If you're a vegan, it might be wise to take note of this warning.

Finally, if for whatever reason you feel you just don't need to take B-12 supplements, be sure to have your blood checked at least once a year.

A BALANCED VEGAN DIET

As in all diets, carnivorous or vegetarian, a balanced diet is essential. The four food groups for a vegan are: grains, legumes and nuts, vegetables, and fruits. Of these, the vegan should emphasize grains in his or her diet, especially whole-wheat breads. But he should scrupulously avoid depending too heavily on any one of the groups. By continually choosing the widest possible variety from the four vegan food groups, a vegan can ensure that he will be getting adequate amounts of all necessary nutrients for good health. Some guidelines to follow for a balanced diet include: Eat at least one serving per day of dark, leafy vegetables; eat three pieces of fruit or drink two glasses of fresh fruit juice daily; work in four or five

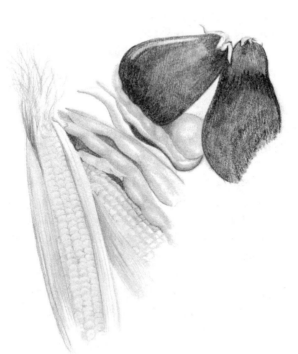

helpings of whole-grain foods, such as a cup of rice, a plate of pasta, two slices of whole-wheat bread, or a half a dozen crackers; and, finally, eat three generous servings of protein foods, such as beans, soy milk, nuts, peanut butter, and tofu.

Here are a few other things a vegan should keep in mind.

Riboflavin is another hard-to-get vitamin for a vegan because it is supplied in most vegetarian diets by milk and eggs. A vegan can get his daily requirement of riboflavin from dark-green vegetables and, also, asparagus, okra, winter squash, and broccoli. Also, calcium and iron, two prominent nutrients also found in milk, can be found in lettuce, turnips, collards, kale, and mustard. Finally, if you don't get enough sunshine, obtaining enough vitamin

D can be a problem. Egg yolk, fortified milk, fish, and liver are the normal dietary sources of vitamin D. But since these are not on a vegan's table, the best answer is to get outdoors more often. Or, if you're a shut-in, a convalescent, or pregnant, you may want to take a vitamin D supplement.

The Lacto-Vegetarian Diet

Unlike the vegan diet, the lacto-vegetarian diet is relatively easy to plan for nutritionally. Milk is important in the diet because it provides protein, calcium, riboflavin, and just about every other essential nutrient. Milk is also easy to assimilate. In countries like Sweden, Denmark, Britain, and Australia, where life expectancy is among the highest in the world, the per-capita consumption of milk is four times higher than in the United States.

The lacto-vegetarian diet, however, is not all peaches and cream. The biggest hazard of lacto-vegetarianism is not whether you'll get enough protein or nutrients from a diet lacking in flesh foods, but whether you'll overcompensate for your fear of not getting enough. This sometimes causes lacto-vegetarians and lacto-ovo-vegetarians to consume huge amounts of fat, which leads to heart disease, liver cirrhosis, and many other complications usually associated with a meat-centered diet.

Fats suffocate tissues by cutting off the oxygen supply, raising the level of cholesterol, and slowing down carbohydrate metabolism. To be safe, then, keep your fat intake below 15 percent of your diet. Do so by limiting or at least carefully watching your consumption of fatty foods, especially whole milk and cheese (Cheddar cheese is the fattiest of all cheeses); nuts such as walnuts, cashews, and peanuts; mayonnaise, butter, margarine, and salad dressing. One of the problems when trying to limit your fat consumption is avoiding "disguised" fats. Peanut butter contains 50 percent fat, nuts have 60 percent, and cheese is 35 percent. Pie and ice cream contain as much as 20 percent fat.

There are other problems associated with an excessive intake of milk. A dairy cow, like a beef steer, lives its life under conditions of the modern factory farm, which includes force-feeding, hormone-laced feed, and regular doses of antibiotics. Even more dangerous than these problems is pesticide residue, since the chlorinated hydrocarbons used in most insecticides accumulate in the fat storage system of the animal. Milk is, of course, made of fat, and the higher the fat content of a dairy product (for example, butter is very high), the higher the concentrations of pesticide residues.

The Lacto-Ovo-Vegetarian Diet

The lacto-ovo-vegetarian diet is one I do not recommend. The yolk of the egg is the single highest source of cholesterol in the average American diet, as well as a source of highly saturated fats. Eating two eggs a day can dangerously increase your serum cholesterol, and remember that eggs are contained in many preprepared frozen entrées.

Crank Diets

I knew a girl who had read about a certain yogi in India who lived only on fruit that dropped from the trees and bushes. To him, only fruit that was given up freely by the plant was God's gift to eat. In this way, the yogi avoided all killing of both animals and plants.

That is a noble reasoning, indeed, and a lovely senti-ment, but as the young lady discovered when she took up this diet, one major problem soon developed—starvation. She spent long hours looking hungrily out at her fruit trees wondering when dinner would be delivered. Fre-quently, it wasn't.

There's one simple guideline to follow in avoiding crank diets. Go with your own good common sense. Avoid a diet that consists of one food only, or whose final goal is the consumption of one food only. The most com-monsense approach to any diet is to eat a wide variety of wholesome, naturally grown foods.

Vegetarianism has often gotten a bad name from peo-ple who are not sensible about their diets. They take it to unwarranted extremes. Don't be a zealot. And don't fol-low someone whose zeal to live a "right" life or cleanse his soul or body of all impurities leads him to malnutri-tion. The one thing to keep in mind is that the life of a human is fraught with imperfection. We all die. The ob-ject of vegetarianism is not to live forever, but to live with health and happiness.

Part Five

GOING VEGETARIAN PHASE TWO: MAKING YOUR VEGETARIAN DIET WORK

Shopping for Vegetarian Foods

If you expect to maintain a vegetarian diet, you're going to have to reeducate yourself a little. A meat-and-potatoes man doesn't have to have a lot of knowledge to satisfy his tastes. A vegetarian, however, owes it to himself to learn about the hundreds of varieties of vegetables, fruits, grains, legumes, nuts, and seeds that are the staples of his diet. He's got to know where to buy them, how to select those of highest quality, and how to prepare them.

Where to Shop

Many items in a sound vegetarian diet are only available at health-food stores. Try to find such a store that packages bulk goods like grains, nuts, seeds, flours, dried fruit, and powdered milk on the premises. Or a store where you're able to weigh out the desired amount of these items and bag them yourself. Hunt around until you find a health-food store you like, and, if it's inconvenient to get there often, buy products in bulk that store well. Foods such as nuts and flours can be kept in the freezer.

Shop at a supermarket if you can buy the same foods of the same quality that you get in the health-food store. The prices will usually be more reasonable.

Finally, look around for a place where you can buy produce grown by local farmers. Fresh fruits and vegetables are worth the effort to find.

What to Look For

Generally, foods are better nutritionally when they are natural and unprocessed. For example, most fruits and vegetables are best eaten raw. When buying food that must be processed, choose those that are the least affected in the processing. Start reading labels to see just what additives are in what products.

Also, buy produce that's in season. Not only will it be fresher, it will be cheaper. If something you normally buy is on special offer, stock up on it if it stores well or can be frozen for future use.

Think twice before buying convenience foods. Steaming or stir-frying vegetables really doesn't take much more time, and is worth the added minutes. When cooking things like beans or grains, make extra and freeze them so they'll be readily available. Also, when you do take the time to cook dishes like casseroles, you may want to make an extra quantity and freeze it.

Grains

Buy whole grains. They contain protein, minerals, vitamins B and E, and are a good source of fiber. However, remember that refining them removes most of the nutrition.

RICE comes in various forms. Brown rice is preferable to white because it is a whole grain.

MILLET is good in soups, stews, and as a rice substitute. It has a sweet flavor and makes a good breakfast cereal.

BARLEY is also good cooked in soups and stews. Cracked barley is called barley grits.

BUCKWHEAT can be used as a rice substitute or as a cereal. Cracked buckwheat is also called buckwheat grits or kasha.

TRITICALE is high in protein and combines well with other grains.

OATS are most commonly found in the form of rolled oats. These are oats that have been steamed and passed through rollers. Use them in cereals and baking.

WHEAT: *Whole-wheat berries* are the grains of whole wheat and can be cooked as a rice substitute, or soaked and used in baking bread. *Bulgur* is a cracked whole wheat that has been partially cooked. It is good in soups, stews, and casseroles, or can be used in salads after soaking. *Cracked wheat* is whole wheat that has been cracked but not cooked.

113

RYE is a whole grain that can be cooked or sprouted.

OTHER GRAIN PRODUCTS

FLOURS: Choose from any of the above whole-grain flours. Most common, of course, is whole wheat. You may want to purchase a little "unbleached" white flour to add to whole-wheat flour for a lighter texture when making bread, although it is not necessary.

BRAN: This is the outer coating of the wheat kernel and is the residue when whole wheat is ground. It is a good source of fiber.

WHEAT GERM: This is the embryo of the wheat, which is also refined out when whole wheat is made into white flour. Use it in cereals, baked goods, casseroles, and soups.

PASTA: Choose from a wide variety of pastas, such as spaghetti, fettucine, linguine, manicotti, macaroni, and lasagne. Also, purchase Chinese-style noodles to top with steamed or stir-fried vegetables.

BREAD: Buy bread made from whole grains and sweetened with honey or molasses. Choose from a wide variety of tastes (like rye or pumpernickel) and shapes (like pita bread or chapatis).

STORAGE OF GRAINS

Refrigerate flours or even freeze them. Also refrigerate raw wheat germ and rolled oats. Pasta should be well packaged, and can be refrigerated if you plan to store it for a while. Grains like rice and millet can be stored in sealed jars, unrefrigerated. Because whole-grain breads are generally free of preservatives, store them in the refrigerator or freezer.

Legumes

Beans, peas, and lentils—or legumes—are sources of protein, minerals, and vitamins. They can be cooked, sprouted, or ground to flour. They are relatively inexpensive and store well. Choose from the wide variety available.

BLACK-EYED PEAS, GREAT NORTHERN BEANS, and NAVY BEANS can all be used in soups and stews.

PINTO BEANS are good in casseroles, as are KIDNEY BEANS, which are commonly used in making chili.

LENTILS make hearty soups and are a good source of iron, cellulose, and B vitamins.

CHICK PEAS (GARBANZO BEANS) are very versatile in the number of good-tasting ways they can be used, and are also high in protein.

SOYBEANS and soybean byproducts are mentioned in the section on "Weird Foods." Your shopping list could include tofu, tamari (for seasoning), soy flour (for baking and in cereals, miso (for soup), and soy milk.

STORAGE OF LEGUMES

Store beans at room temperature in glass jars with tight lids. Tofu should be refrigerated. It keeps best if you put it in a bowl of fresh water and keep replacing the water until you use it.

Nuts and Seeds

Nuts and seeds are sources of protein, minerals, some B vitamins, and unsaturated fatty acids. They can be purchased in shells, but this may be a little inconvenient. It's most practical to buy them shelled and raw. (You can roast them yourself if you wish.)

NUTS: Nuts are a great snack food, but use restraint. Not only are they expensive, but they are a concentrated form of fats and calories. They can also make delicious ingredients in cereals, main dishes, and desserts. Some choices are: *almonds, cashews, pecans, walnuts, pignolias, pistachios, Brazil nuts,* and *peanuts* (although peanuts are actually a legume). Nuts are also available as nut butters, like peanut butter.

SEEDS: The most popular choices are *sunflower seeds, pumpkin seeds,* and *sesame seeds.* See the section on "Weird Foods" for more details on their nutritional benefits.

STORAGE OF NUTS AND SEEDS

Although nuts and seeds can be stored at room temperature for short periods of time, it is preferable to keep them in the refrigerator. If you purchase them in bulk, keep them in the freezer.

Dairy Products

It is well-known that dairy products are an excellent source of protein and calcium. But it's a good idea to be aware of some of the concerns about dairy products and to exercise discretion when buying them.

MILK: Because dairy cows are subject to chemicals in the form of antibiotics and pesticides from eating sprayed plants, milk will also be exposed to these chemicals. Also, many people feel the processes of pasteurization and homogenization deplete the nutrition in milk. Their suggestion is to purchase "certified raw" milk.

POWDERED MILK: If you can, get low-fat, noninstant milk powder, usually available at health-food stores.

BUTTERMILK, YOGURT, and KEFIR are examples of cultured or fermented milk products. They are more easily digested than milk.

COTTAGE CHEESE is both high in protein and low in calories.

CHEESE may be transformed from milk by rennin, an enzyme that is obtained from slaughtered animals. There are "renninless" cheeses available, especially at health-food stores. Read the labels or find out from the processors if their cheeses contain rennin. The labels should also tell you if there are artificial colorings and additives in the cheese. There are cheeses available that are made from raw milk.

RICOTTA CHEESE is a soft cheese similar to cottage cheese. It is not made with rennin.

BUTTER: You can buy "sweet butter," which means it is unsalted. Also, "certified raw" butter is available in some places.

STORAGE OF DAIRY PRODUCTS

Store all of the above in the refrigerator. You may also put your butter and cheeses in the freezer.

Sweeteners

White sugar is probably the most common form of sweetener, but it is so highly refined that it is nothing but calories. Although all sweeteners should be used in moderation, there is a wide variety of natural sweeteners available.

MALT is good in beverages and baked goods and is not as sweet as many other sweeteners. As a rule, it is made from barley.

MOLASSES is a sweetener produced during sugar refining that contains B vitamins, calcium, and iron. Look for unsulfured molasses. *Blackstrap molasses* is rich in minerals, but it has a strong flavor so should be used sparingly.

MAPLE SYRUP is expensive and very sweet. It's delicious, but use in small quantities.

DATE SUGAR is a natural sweetener made from dried ground dates, and is delicious sprinkled on cereals and desserts.

HONEY is available in a wide range of types and tastes. Look for the words "raw," "uncooked," or "unfiltered" on the label. One word of warning! Don't go overboard with honey—it is a sugar.

SORGHUM is a syrup that is made from grain.

RAISINS and DATES are great natural sweeteners.

STORAGE OF SWEETENERS

Keep maple syrup refrigerated. Other sweeteners can be stored in glass containers at room temperature.

Oils

Try to buy pure, unrefined vegetable oils that will still contain nutrients. Look for the words "pressed" and "unrefined" on the label. Different oils have different tastes. You can choose from a variety of oils, including *soybean oil, safflower oil, sunflower oil, corn oil, peanut oil, sesame oil,* and *olive oil.*

STORAGE OF OILS

Keep oils in a cool place or refrigerate them.

Fruits and Vegetables

Although the next chapter includes an entire list of fresh fruits and vegetables and how to select them, here are a few canned or frozen items you may want to include on your shopping list.

Frozen spinach: This can be used in making dishes like spinach lasagna. When eating spinach either lightly steamed or raw in a salad, always use fresh spinach. But when cooked in a casserole, especially in fairly large amounts, it's much more practical to use frozen spinach.

Canned tomatoes, tomato sauce, and *tomato paste:* Although it is preferable to buy fresh tomatoes and make your own sauce, sometimes the quality and the cost make it more practical to purchase canned tomatoes and sauces. Check the ingredients on the label to get those with the least amount of additives.

Miscellaneous Foods

EGG SUBSTITUTE: This is mentioned in some of the recipes. It is commercially made and serves the purpose of eggs in baked goods. "Jolly Joan" is a dependable brand.

VEGETABLE BOUILLON CUBES are convenient to use as a base for soups or gravies.

Weird Foods, or What'll I Do with This Bag of Tofu?

The Soybean and Its Relatives

Soybeans are well-known as a high-quality, inexpensive source of dietary protein. They are also a healthy source of protein, since they are cholesterol-free and are rich in B vitamins, calcium, phosphorus, iron, and potassium. The beans can be used in soups and casseroles, mashed into spreads, ground into burgers, and roasted as snacks.

TOFU (also known as bean curd or soy bean cake) is high in protein, yet low in saturated fats and free of cholesterol. High in nutrition, yet low in calories, tofu is easily digestible and has a mild taste that will take on the flavor of whatever it is mixed with. Made into soups, stews, casseroles, salad dressings, and even desserts, its uses are limited only by the imagination.

SOY MILK is produced when the soybean is ground and cooked with water. Because it is high in protein, it has significant advantages for vegans, and for those who are allergic to dairy products, especially if it is fortified with vitamin B-12 and calcium. It can be made fresh, or purchased canned or powdered. It has a unique flavor, and may be substituted in any recipe that calls for dairy milk.

SOY FLOUR is made from finely ground raw soybeans. It is a good source of protein, and combines particularly well with other flours to enrich baked goods.

SOY GRITS are made from defatted soy flour. They are granular and can often be used in recipes to replace bread crumbs or ground nuts.

TAMARI is a naturally fermented soy sauce, made with soybeans, wheat, and sea salt, and aged in wooden casks.

MISO is a fermented soybean paste, which can be used like tamari in some dishes or as a base for soups.

TEMPEH is a cultured cake of cooked soybeans with a mild taste and cheeselike texture. It can be fried, roasted, or broiled, and served in soups, salads, sandwiches, and main dishes.

OKARA is the pulverized outer layer of the soybean that is left after the soy milk is strained out of the ground beans. It rivals bran as a source of fiber, and is also high in protein. Like tofu, its uses are varied, and it can be an ingredient in burgers, soups, casseroles, and even baked goods.

Other Weird Foods

ARROWROOT is a powder or flour made from the arrowroot plant, and is a natural thickening agent. It is used instead of cornstarch, which is a refined food and apt to be treated with sulfur dioxide in processing.

BREWER'S YEAST or NUTRITIONAL YEAST is a good source of protein, minerals, and B vitamins, including B-12. The taste is strong, so it may take some experimenting with the variety of brands available to find the most palatable to you. If used discreetly in things like soups and casseroles, it will add nutrition without affecting taste.

CAROB POWDER is ground from carob pods and used as a chocolate substitute. It is a source of calcium, minerals, and natural sugars. Unlike chocolate, it is low in fat and does not contain theobromine, a stimulant similar to caffeine. It is also called St. John's Bread, because it is said St. John lived on carob while in the desert.

LECITHIN GRANULES and LECITHIN LIQUID are soybean by-products. Recent research has shown that lecithin may help lower serum cholesterol levels. The granules, also called "soy phosphatides," can be added to cereal, soup, or liquids. Liquid lecithin can be mixed into drinks, or mixed with vegetable oil to replace part of the oil for cooking or baking, or to make salad dressing.

PUMPKIN SEEDS are a source of protein, phosphorus, iron, and zinc, and are rich in unsaturated fat.

SEAWEEDS are a source of all the trace minerals required by the body for nutrition. They contain iodine, sodium, iron, calcium, magnesium, potassium, and phosphorus. Some of the more commonly used forms are kelp, dulse, and agar.

Kelp is one of the brown seaweeds and has an excellent mineral content. It is a principal source of iodine, and is available in granules or as a powder or tablet.

Dulse is one of the red seaweeds and comes from the

Atlantic Ocean. It is usually eaten dried or raw, and can be added to soups and salads.

Agar or *agar-agar* is an extract of seaweed that can be used to thicken juices. It serves the same jelling function as gelatin, but contains no animal sources. It usually comes in three forms: powder, flakes, and bars called kantan.

SESAME SEEDS are a good source of calcium and protein, and contain lecithin, vitamin E, B vitamins, and unsaturated fatty acids. They are available either hulled or unhulled.

SUNFLOWER SEEDS are a source of protein, iron, magnesium, potassium, zinc, phosphorus, and unsaturated fatty acids. They also can be purchased ground up into a meal, which can be used like wheat germ.

TAHINI or SESAME BUTTER is a paste made from ground sesame seeds, which can be used as a spread or mixed into other dishes.

TAPIOCA is made from the cassava plant and can be purchased whole or pearled. It is most popular when made into a pudding. Tapioca flour is a natural thickening agent.

WHEAT GERM is the embryo of the wheat and a good source of protein, riboflavin, thiamin, and vitamin E. When making white flour from whole wheat, it is the wheat germ and the bran that are refined out. It is available both raw and toasted. Refrigerate raw wheat germ to guard against rancidity. It can be mixed with cereal, combined in casseroles and baked goods, or sprinkled on other foods as desired.

YOGURT is a cultured milk product with the same quality of protein as milk. It is easier to digest than milk, because the "friendly" bacteria that ferment the yogurt also predigest the lactose. It is best homemade or purchased plain. It can be used in blender drinks, salad dressing, substituted for sour cream in recipes, or mixed with fruit and nuts.

Selecting Fruits and Vegetables

Vegetables

ARTICHOKES: High in nutrition, low in calories, and a good source of vitamins A, B-1, and riboflavin.

How to select: good green color, tightly packed leaves, firm leaf stalks. Taste bears no relation to size. The stalks are also edible.

Storage: Use as soon as possible or store in refrigerator up to four days.

Basic preparation: Cut stem ½ to ¼ inch below vegetable. Remove tough outer leaves near base. Trim tips of leaves with scissors. Wash well in cold water to remove grit hidden in leaves. To prevent oxidation, rub with lemon or submerge in lemon water with a few drops of oil added to cooking water.

ASPARAGUS: High in vitamins A, B, C, and riboflavin. The stalks are high in roughage.

How to select: Select firm, bright-green, rounded stalks with compact tips. Avoid flat stalks and open heads.

Storage: Asparagus loses sugar quickly so use as soon as possible. Store in plastic bag in refrigerator up to four days.

Basic preparation: Wash in water, snap or cut off woody ends. Can be steamed or boiled.

BEANS (Green or Snap or Yellow): High in vitamins A, B, C. Rich in potassium.

How to select: Beans should be young and crisp, without bulges, bumps or rust spots. If beans are hard, they have been on the vine too long.

Storage: Store unwashed in crisper or plastic bags up to five days. Use as soon as possible.

Basic preparation: Wash and cut off ends. Leave whole or snap or cut into 1-inch pieces.

BEETS: Vitamins A, B, and riboflavin. High in sodium, potassium, and magnesium.

How to select: Beets should have a rich, dark-red color with no wet spots or ridges, and should be relatively smooth. Beet tops should be fresh and green.

Storage: Store in plastic bag or vegetable crisper up to two weeks. Remove tops, leaving tips on beets.

Basic preparation: Wash thoroughly. Cook with skin and tips on beet. After cooking, peel skin and tips off; this prevents red color from running out.

BEET TOPS (leaves): May be used like spinach, or young leaves may be used in a salad. High in thiamine, riboflavin, and vitamin C.

BROCCOLI: Low in sodium, high in vitamins A, B-1, and C, potassium, calcium, sulfur, and roughage.

How to select: Choose bright-green stalks with compact heads. Stalks should not be thick and heavy. The thinner the shoots, the more even the cooking time.

Storage: Keep in vegetable crisper or plastic bag up to one week.

127

Basic preparation: Wash thoroughly in cold water. Trim off leaves and end of stalk. If stalks are heavy, split up stem to flower head. Broccoli is best steamed and not overcooked as it then becomes soggy and loses its color.

BRUSSELS SPROUTS: High in vitamins A, B, and C.

How to select: Choose small to medium firm, compact sprouts. There should be no yellow leaves or worm holes.

Storage: Up to four days in plastic bag or crisper in refrigerator.

Basic preparation: Remove wilted or discolored outer leaves and trim tip of stem. Wash well. Good steamed or cooked in very little water for about 6 to 8 minutes. Do not overcook.

CABBAGE (Green or Red): High in vitamins B-2 and C, and potassium. Low in calories and high in roughage.

How to select: Choose compact, firm heads. If outer leaves are wilted, shriveled, or yellowed, avoid them.

Storage: Store one to two weeks in plastic bag in coldest part of refrigerator.

Basic preparation: Remove outer leaves if extra grimy or tough. Trim stem, and core. Cut just before using, as vitamin C is lost after cutting. Cabbage can be cut or shredded, it can be eaten raw or cooked. A very versatile vegetable.

CARROTS: High in vitamins A and B-1, potassium.

How to select: Choose firm, smooth roots. Split and cracked carrots are tough and old.

Storage: Store in cool, dry place or vegetable crisper; in plastic bag one to two weeks.

Basic preparation: Remove tips and leaves to stalk. Clean well with vegetable scrubber or peel if skin is older. Can be eaten raw or cooked.

CAULIFLOWER: High in vitamins B-1 and C, iron. Low in calories.

How to select: Choose firm, compact heads and flowerets with even white color and fresh, bright-green leaves.

Storage: Store three to five days in plastic bag in refrigerator.

Basic preparation: Remove green leaves and trim base. Wash in cold water and shake out. Repeat the washing. Can be eaten raw or cooked.

CELERY: High in vitamins A and B-1, phosphorus and calcium. High in sodium and roughage. Very low in calories.

How to select: Choose thick, crisp stalks with fresh green tops. Avoid rusty discoloration.

Storage: Tightly wrap in plastic bags and store in coldest part of refrigerator up to five days. Stand in cold water in refrigerator if necessary.

Basic preparation: Cut tops and base off celery. Wash and scrub clean in cold water. Tops can be dried or used fresh, great in soups or stews. Top and trimmings can be used for making vegetable stocks.

CHARD: Vitamins A, B-1, and C, iron and sulfur.

How to select: Crisp tender leaves.

Storage: Up to two days in plastic bag in refrigerator.

Basic preparation: Use leaves like spinach. Wash well to remove grit. Separate stems and cook separately. Good steamed.

CORN: A, magnesium, copper, niacin, riboflavin, thiamine, and phosphorus.

How to select: Choose fresh green husks, with stem ends that are not dried out. Always buy corn with husks on. Corn loses sugar immediately on harvesting, so use as soon as possible. Kernels should be plump with a light yellow color, never shrunken or dented.

Storage: if you can't use immediately, store unhusked in plastic bags in refrigerator up to two days.

Basic preparation: Remove husks and silk just before cooking. Rinse well. Do not overcook as corn becomes tough. Really fresh corn need be cooked only about 3 minutes in boiling water.

CUCUMBER: Vitamin B-1 and riboflavin. Low in calories.

How to select: Choose firm, small to medium cucumbers, dark green in color, and unwaxed, if you can find them. The wax will not wash off, so peel those that are waxed. Some cucumbers are hydroponically grown and sold wrapped in plastic. These are burpless and seedless and the peel may be eaten. Always wrap cut end in plastic as these tend to deteriorate quickly.

Storage: Refrigerate in plastic bags up to one week.

Basic preparation: Wash and if waxed, peel.

EGGPLANT: Vitamin B-1 and riboflavin.

How to select: Choose firm, glossy, dark purple skins, not spotted or shriveled. Stem should be fresh and green. Avoid soft, dull-looking eggplants—they are too old.

Storage: Store in cool place or in plastic wrap to retain moisture in refrigerator up to two days.

Basic preparation: Wash and cut stem. Can be eaten raw, or peeled and cooked, depending on recipe. Can become mushy if overcooked. Before frying, place pieces under broiler to retard excess oil absorption by eggplant.

LETTUCE (Iceberg, Butterhead, Bibb, Romaine): The darker-leafed varieties contain greater amounts of vitamins A and C and essential minerals.

How to select: Choose heavy, compact heads, with bright-green outer leaves for iceberg. In loose leaf varieties, choose those with dark-green color. Avoid wilted, yellowed, white or hard leaves. These are too old.

Storage: Wash well, don't soak. Store in vegetable cripser or plastic bags in refrigerator up to five days.

Basic preparation: Tear with hands or shred with knife.

MUSHROOMS: High in protein and phosphorus, riboflavin, calcium, and niacin. Some iron and copper. Low in calories.

How to select: Mushrooms should be creamy white to slightly brown. Choose mushroom caps that are more closed than open, not exposing the gills underneath. They should be firm, not spongy. Avoid pitted caps.

Storage: Store in plastic bag or on a plate covered with damp towel in refrigerator up to one week.

Basic preparation: Wipe and trim stalk end.

ONION: Vitamins A and C, calcium and phosphorus, potassium and sulfur.

How to select: Onions should be hard, with dry but not brittle skins. Avoid those with soft spots. Sprouting indicates age. For scallions (green onions), pick fresh, firm stalks with green tops and small white bulbs.

Storage: Store all onions in a dry, cool, well-ventilated place. Storage in closed plastic bags will make them sprout too quickly. However, for immediate use, store a few in refrigerator in plastic bag to reduce tears while cutting them.

Basic preparation: Trim ends and remove outer skin. You can do this under water to reduce weeping.

PARSNIPS: Vitamin C, calcium, phosphorus, and potassium.

How to select: Choose small to medium bulbs, smooth and firm, and uniform in size. Larger bulbs are usually tough.

Storage: In refrigerator up to one week.

Basic preparation: For a nutty, sweet flavor, steam in peel. Remove after cooking. Do not boil in peel.

PEAS (Green): Vitamins A and C, calcium, riboflavin, thiamine, niacin and iron, phosphorus and potassium.

How to select: Pods should be firm, bright green, and crisp, and squeak when rubbed together. Peas begin to lose their sugar immediately on picking, so use as soon as possible.

Storage: Store in pods up to two days in coldest part of refrigerator.

Basic preparation: Leave in pods until ready to use. Shell peas and eat raw, or steam or boil in a little water for 15 minutes. Do not overcook. When they are fresh, peas have a lovely sweet flavor.

PEPPERS (Bell peppers, red and green): High in vitamins A and C.

How to select: Choose firm, smooth, thick flesh, with shiny, strong color (red or green). The red bell pepper is simply the green pepper that has matured on the vine. It contains more vitamin C and is sweeter to the taste. Avoid wrinkled skin or soft spots.

Storage: In crisper or plastic bag in refrigerator for up to one week.

Basic preparation: Trim top, remove inner seeds and membrane, wash.

PARSLEY: Very high in protein and iron. Also high in potassium, vitamins A and C.

How to select: Choose bright-green, crisp leaves, free from yellowing or wilting.

Storage: Wash and store in plastic bag in refrigerator up to one week. May be chopped and placed in freezer for future use.

Basic preparation: Wash, trim tough ends. Mince, chop, or cut with scissors.

POTATOES: High in vitamin C, iron, potassium, niacin, and phosphorus.

How to select: Should be firm and smooth without cracks, eyes, green spots, or soft spots.

Storage: Should be stored in a cool, dark, well-ventilated place.

Basic preparation: Scrub well with vegetable brush. Cook in skins. May remove skins after cooking.

SWEET POTATOES (Yams): Very high in vitamin A, phosphorus, calcium, potassium.

How to select: Chose firm, well-shaped roots. Yams should be moist with bright orange color. Sweet potatoes should be dry, and a light yellow to tan color. Potatoes should have no cuts or surface injury.

Storage: Store in dry, cool, well-ventilated place. Do not refrigerate. Can be stored for several months.

Basic preparation: Scrub well. Should be boiled or baked with skins on to retain vitamins and to keep potatoes from bleeding their syrup.

RADISHES: Vitamin C, iron, sulfur, phosphorus, calcium, sodium, potassium.

How to select: Choose firm, smooth, well-rounded

roots, with bright color. Soft, spongy roots or yellowed, wilted tops indicate age.

Storage: Remove tops. Place in plastic bag in refrigerator up to two weeks.

Basic preparation: Wash well, trim roots and leaves.

SPINACH: Vitamins A and C, potassium, riboflavin, calcium, iron.

How to select: Spinach should have bright-green color and tender leaves. Avoid wilted or yellowed leaves.

Storage: Wash well. Drain and store in crisper or in plastic bag up to five days.

Basic preparation: Spinach usually has a considerable amount of grit hidden in leaves. Best method of cleaning is to submerge in water. Fill sink and place spinach in water. Drain well. Remove yellowed or tough leaves; snip stems.

SQUASH (Zucchini, Yellow, Acorn, Summer, Banana): High in vitamin A.

How to select: In general, all squash should have good color, firm body, and smooth rind. Zucchini and summer squash have a softened rind, while winter, acorn, and butternut have a thicker rind.

Storage: Store zucchini and summer squash in plastic bag in refrigerator up to one week. Store butternut and acorn squash in dry, cool place.

Basic preparation: For zucchini and summer squash, do not peel. Trim ends. For hard-rinded squash cut in half, scoop out seeds, and bake in rind. Do not eat rind.

TOMATO: High in vitamins A and C, phosphorus, sodium, potassium, calcium.

How to select: Ripe tomatoes should have strong color. Skins should be plump and smooth with no cracks or soft spots.

Storage: Store red, ripe tomatoes in refrigerator up to

four days. Green tomatoes need to ripen at room temperature out of direct light.

Basic preparation: Wash, remove core.

TURNIPS: Vitamin C, phosphorus, sodium, calcium, potassium.

How to select: Turnips should be smooth and firm, with green tops. Should have some root attached.

Storage: Store in plastic bag in refrigerator for up to one month.

Basic preparation: Scrub, trim ends, peel and cut to eat raw. Or add to soups and stews.

Fruits

APPLES: High in A and C, calcium, thiamine, phosphorus, potassium.

How to select: Apples should be crisp and firm, with no bruises, holes, or soft spots. Color should be fully developed.

Storage: Keep in dry, cool place. Plastic wrap speeds deterioration.

Basic preparation: Since most commercial apples are waxed, it is best to peel them. Most of the important vitamins and nutrients are stored just under the skin, so removal of peel shouldn't alter nutritional value.

APRICOTS: High in vitamin A and C, iron, potassium, phosphorus, calcium.

How to select: Apricots should have a golden-yellow to orange-yellow color. Fruit should be soft and plump. Wrinkled skin indicates age. You may select hard, unripened fruit to ripen at home.

Storage: Ripe apricots should be used as soon as possible. Unripe fruit should be kept at room temperature until ripe, then refrigerated.

AVOCADO: Vitamin A, riboflavin, niacin, calcium, potassium, thiamine. High fat content.

How to select: Ripe avocadoes give slightly under pressure. Avoid mushy, bruised fruit. Choose a dark purple or, for smooth-skinned avocadoes, a dull green color for ripe fruit.

Storage: If ripe, store in refrigerator. After avocados are cut they oxidize quickly, so wrap tightly. Unripened fruit should be stored at room temperature, or placed in a paper bag or foil to speed up the process.

Basic preparation: Peel or cut in half and remove pit. Sprinkle with lemon juice to prevent darkening.

BANANAS: Vitamin A, potassium, calcium, iron, phosphorus.

How to select: Choose fruit that's firm and sunny yellow with brown spots. The brown spots indicate that the starch has turned to sugar and the banana is ready to eat. Green bananas may be selected to ripen at home.

Storage: Ripe bananas may be kept in the refrigerator after they are fully ripened. The cold decelerates maturing process. Skins may turn black but fruit is fine to eat. You may also freeze ripe bananas. Wrap in plastic or foil and use in blender drinks. Green bananas must be stored at room temperature until ripened.

BLUEBERRIES: Vitamins A and C, iron, manganese, potassium, phosphorus, calcium.

How to select: Firm and even in color.

Storage: Store in well-ventilated container in refrigerator, or freeze in double plastic bags up to one year.

Basic preparation: Wash and refrigerate or freeze.

BLACKBERRIES: Vitamins A and C, calcium, phosphorus, potassium.

How to select: Must be dead black in color before fully ripened. Should be firm but not hard.

Storage: When ripe, store in well-ventilated container in refrigerator. You may freeze in double plastic bag, up to one year.

Basic preparation: Wash and refrigerate or freeze.

CHERRIES: Vitamins A and C, copper, iron, manganese, phosphorus, potassium, calcium.

How to select: Should be plump and firm and almost black in color.

Storage: Store in well-ventilated container in refrigerator. May also freeze in double plastic bags up to one year.

COCONUTS: Potassium, sodium, iron.

How to select: Choose a nut that is heavy, with a hard shell. Shake to make sure it's full of milk.

Storage: Store both meat and milk in refrigerator. Grated coconut keeps several days in the refrigerator and indefinitely in the freezer.

Basic preparation: To open, push a nail or screwdriver through the eye of nut. Drain milk and refrigerate. With hammer, rap nut on one of the ridges running lengthwise until it opens. Or bake in oven heated to 300° for about 1 hour, or until it cracks easily with a hammer. Use a sharp knife to remove meat and a peeler to remove brown bits of shell clinging to meat. You may dry grated coconut in oven at 150° for 3 to 4 hours.

CRANBERRIES: Vitamin C, potassium, calcium, phosphorus.

How to select: Choose bright-colored plump berries.

Storage: Store in plastic bag in refrigerator.

Basic preparation: Because these berries have such a short season, buy a couple of bags and put them in the freezer for use in muffins, breads, and jellies.

GRAPES: Vitamins A and C, potassium, low in sodium.

How to select: Firm, plump, brightly colored, with green stems.

137

Storage: Refrigerate in plastic bags up to one week. May freeze up to one year.

GRAPEFRUIT (Pink and White): Vitamins A (higher in pink) and C, phosphorus, potassium, calcium.

How to select: Choose firm, heavy fruit. Avoid spongy fruit. A thinner rind may indicate juicier fruit.

Storage: Store in plastic bag in refrigerator up to one month.

LEMONS and LIMES: Vitamins A and C, potassium, calcium, phosphorus.

How to select: Rinds should be firm, brightly colored, and fine-textured. Avoid large-pored, mushy fruit with wrinkled skin.

Storage: Store in vegetable crisper or freezer.

Basic preparation: To cash in on seasonal bargain prices, juice fruit and freeze juice in ice-cube trays. When frozen, store in plastic bags. Use in mineral waters, carbonated drinks, and juices.

MANGOES: Vitamins A and C, niacin, potassium, iodine, phosphorus, calcium, sodium.

How to select: Mangoes come in many colors from green to yellow-orange to reddish yellow. Choose a rich tint and go more by feel. Mangoes should yield to slight pressure but should not be mushy. Avoid mangoes that have spots.

Storage: In refrigerator, or if not quite ripe, at room temperature for a few days.

Basic preparation: Peel and eat raw. Or use in fruit salad. Excellent in fruit breads and muffins. Mango bread is very popular in Hawaii.

MELONS (Canteloupes, Persian, Water, Crenshaw, Casaba, Honeydew): Vitamins A and C.

How to select: Choose firm fruit. Avoid melons with soft spots or soggy ends. Since there are quite a few varieties of melons, ask your grocer if you're not sure about ripeness.

Storage: After cutting, enclose in plastic bag and refrigerate up to one week.

NECTARINES: Vitamins A and C, calcium, potassium, phosphorus.

How to select: Choose firm but not hard fruit. Colors are reddish, yellow, and orange combinations. Avoid green, bruised fruit.

Storage: Store at room temperature. Or peel, cut in half or in quarters, remove stone, and freeze in plastic bags.

ORANGES: Vitamins A and C, phosphorus, calcium, potassium.

How to select: Smooth rinds, brightly colored. Avoid soft, mushy rinds.

Storage: Store in a dry, cool place.

PAPAYAS: High in vitamins A, B, D, twice as much vitamin C as oranges.

How to select: Green papayas are not ripe. Choose a firm papaya with as much light yellow color as possible.

Storage: Store in refrigerator for a few days.

Basic preparation: Cut in half and scoop out seeds. Papayas have a natural cup where seeds have been held. Fill this cup with yogurt or cottage cheese. Also eat plain, with a squirt of lemon or lime. Puréed papaya can be used in muffins or bread. To purée, peel papaya, seed, and cut into chunks. Place chunks in blender, and blend until smooth.

PEACHES: Vitamins A and C, potassium, niacin.

How to select: Choose firm fruits with light creamy yellow color. Reddish tints do not necessarily denote ripeness. Avoid hard green fruits.

Storage: Store in vegetable crisper for a few days.

PEARS: Vitamins A and C.

How to select: Depending on variety, pears should have light yellow coloring (Bartlett pear) or light brown with some russeting (Bosc pear). Deep yellow indicates a very ripe to overripe pear. Pears should be firm but tender. Avoid soft spots, or mushy fruit. You may buy unripened fruit to ripen at home.

Storage: Store unripened fruit in plastic or paper bag in cool place. Ripe fruit should be stored in the refrigerator.

PINEAPPLES: Vitamin C, potassium.

How to select: Choose a firm, golden yellow fruit with fresh green leaves. Pineapples do not ripen after they are picked. Avoid green, bruised fruit, with dried-out leaves.

Storage: Cut out the fruit and store in the refrigerator.

Basic preparation: Pineapples have a hard core in the center, which should be discarded. You may slice the pineapple in half, removing fruit from shell. Core the pineapple, mix the fruit with other chopped seasonal fruits, and return to shell for a fresh fruit dessert.

PLUMS: Vitamins A, calcium, potassium, iron.

How to select: Choose plump, firm fruit. Plums come in a variety of colors. Choose rich, deep colors. Avoid bruised, split, or hard plums.

Storage: Fruit should be ripened at room temperature. Keep ripe plums in refrigerator.

STRAWBERRIES: Vitamins A and C, phosphorus, iron, calcium.

How to select: Choose firm, bright-red berries. Berries should have their green caps attached, since strawberries start to lose their vitamin C as soon as these are removed.

Storage: Refrigerate. Don't wash or take off caps before using.

TANGERINES: Vitamins A and C, potassium, phosphorus, calcium.

How to select: Choose fruit with deep orange color.

Storage: Refrigerate in vegetable crisper.

The Basic Preparation of Vegetarian Foods

Basic Cooking of Vegetables

Since vegetables will comprise a great deal of your diet, it's essential to become familiar with the various rules of cooking and preparing them.

No matter what the preparation, in cooking we are concerned mostly with retaining all or most of the essential vitamins and nutrients contained in the vegetables. The usual methods of cooking in the past have involved overcleaning and overcooking the vegetables.

The three basic ways of cooking vegetables for the best flavor and nutrition are steaming, stir-frying or sautéing, and oven-baking.

STEAMING

You steam vegetables by using a steaming basket placed in a pan with a few inches of water. The pan is covered with a tight-fitting lid. The advantage of steam-

142

ing is that the vegetables can be cooked, whole or cut, in a very short time. The vegetables keep their true colors and textures, and retain their vitamins and minerals. In conventional cooking, most of the nutrients are boiled away—the important vitamins and minerals are leached into the cooking water, which is thrown away.

Most root vegetables like carrots, potatoes, and beets store their vitamins and minerals in and directly under their skins. Scrub the skins well with a vegetable brush. If they are especially grimy, you can scrape the skins lightly with a knife or vegetable peeler.

When cooking a combination of vegetables, place the tougher vegetables such as carrots, broccoli, and cauliflower in the steamer first. Steam a few minutes, then add the rest of the vegetables in descending order of toughness—tomatoes, zucchini, mushrooms, etc. Be sure to keep an eye on the water supply under the basket when cooking a lot of vegetables. Don't let all the water boil off and permit the vegetables to get scorched.

Here are a few points to remember when steaming vegetables:

1. Fill pot with 1 or 2 inches of water. Don't let water boil over the vegetables in the steamer basket.
2. Let the water come to a boil first, then add the vegetables. Lower the temperature to prevent rapid evaporation of water from the pot.

3. Don't overcook the vegetables. Cook them until just tender and serve immediately.
4. The left-over liquid from steaming can be used in soups, vegetable drinks, stocks, and sauces. Freeze the liquid in ice-cube trays or plastic containers for future use.

STEAMING: COOKING TIME

Artichokes	18–20	minutes
Asparagus	8–12	"
Beans (string)	7–10	"
Beets, sliced	6–8	"
Broccoli	6–8	"
Brussels sprouts	11–14	"
Cabbage, quartered	10–15	"
Carrots, sliced	6–8	"
Cauliflower, quartered	12–15	"
Celery	8–10	"
Corn on the cob	5–6	"
Mushrooms	6–9	"
Peas	6–8	"
Potatoes, small whole	14–18	"
Spinach	8–10	"
Tomatoes	4–5	"
Zucchini, sliced	5–7	"

STIR-FRYING OR SAUTÉEING

Stir-frying or sautéeing is best done in a Chinese wok or a large cast-iron skillet. You heat the wok or pan, add a little oil, wait until it gets hot, then drop in the prepared vegetables. Stir-toss them until just tender. If you wish, you may cook the tougher vegetables first, adding the softer vegetables after a few minutes. As you become more familiar with this method of cooking, you will notice how versatile it is. You can change the flavor of your meals by adding olive oil and herbs, or sprinkling tamari and chili oil over the vegetables.

OVEN-BAKING

Prepare the vegetables the same as you would for steaming or stir-frying. In fact, you can precook them by quickly stir-frying and then placing them in a casserole in the oven. This is a slower way of cooking vegetables, but you have the advantage of cooking them in whatever sauces, spices, and herbs you like, to achieve different tastes. These casseroles can be topped off with cheese and bread crumbs.

EQUIPMENT

A word about equipment because there are a few pieces that will make your life a lot easier in the kitchen. Useful are:

1. Good sharp knives for cutting and paring.
2. A vegetable peeler and a vegetable scrub brush.
3. A steamer basket and two 6-quart Dutch ovens with lids (these are for soup-making, spaghetti-making, and steaming; the ones with the copper bottoms are good because they distribute the heat more evenly).
4. A blender is hard to be without, once you get used to one—use it for making soups, smooth drinks, and desserts; for chopping nuts, grinding seeds, and mincing vegetables.
5. A Chinese wok for stir-frying and steaming, and a cast-iron skillet for frying and sautéeing. (The cast iron adds valuable iron to the diet.)
6. Pressure cookers can cut down on the soaking and cooking times of beans and grains.

Teflon- and silverstone-coated skillets, pans, and cookie sheets can be a real help, but be careful choosing them. Some of the cheaper brands tend to chip and flake off. Also, be careful of cookware made from aluminum, as this can be a toxic material. The best materials for cookware are made of cast iron, stainless steel, baked enamel, glass, and earthenware.

Basic Cooking of Grains

1. Wash grains thoroughly.
2. In cooking grains, generally use about two parts water to one part grain. You can use a vegetable broth instead of water to flavor the grain. Or you can add herbs to the cooking liquid.
3. There are basically three different ways to cook grains:
    a) Put the water and grain in a pan and bring to a boil. Stir. Cover and turn down the heat to simmer. Cook until the grain is tender and the water is absorbed. Don't take the lid off during cooking, and don't stir the grain again.
    b) Bring water to a boil, and add grain slowly so the water keeps boiling. Stir, cover, lower heat, and cook until grain is tender.
    c) Before cooking, toast the grain for a few minutes in a heavy frying pan, or sauté the grain in a little oil, stirring frequently. When the grain is browned, add hot water, bring to a boil, lower heat, cover, and simmer.
4. Cooking times will vary with each grain. Brown rice generally takes about 45 minutes. Cracked grains, bulgur, and millet take about 20 minutes. Whole-wheat berries, whole rye, and triticale take over an hour. Rolled oats take only about 10 minutes. If you are using a pressure cooker, the cooking time will be considerably less.

Basic Cooking of Beans

Allow about ¼ to ⅓ cup of dry beans per serving. Most beans approximately double in bulk when cooked, although soybeans may increase up to three times in volume.

1. Wash beans carefully.
2. Cover beans with three to four times as much water in a pot.
3. Before cooking, soak the beans in either of two ways:

a) Soak overnight. You may want to refrigerate the beans to prevent fermentation.

b) Bring the beans and water to a boil and simmer for a few minutes. Remove from the heat and let them sit for an hour or two before cooking.

4. If necessary, add water so there is again four times as much water as beans. Put the lid on and simmer until the beans are done. To stop them from foaming, you can add oil to the water (about 1 tablespoon per cup of beans). Stir occasionally. It will usually take from 3 to 5 hours for the beans to become cooked and tender. If you have a pressure cooker, the cooking time will be greatly reduced.

Note: Lentils and split peas cook quite quickly (about 1 hour) and don't have to be presoaked.

5. If you are not using the beans immediately, you can freeze the cooked beans in plastic containers.

Sprouts

Sprouts are a useful food for the vegetarian because they can be "grown" in your own kitchen, ensuring the freshest produce available. Sprouts are grown from any

147

whole dried seeds, beans, peas, or grains. When sprouted, the protein that is locked inside these seeds is predigested, changing the amino acids into a simpler form more easily used by the body. Sprouts are also a good source of roughage, which is essential for the proper function of the intestinal tract.

To grow sprouts, start with good quality seeds. Most health-food stores sell them. Some of the most successful seeds and beans for sprouting are mung, pea, alfalfa, radish, red clover, cabbage, lentil, adzuki, and garbanzo. Do not use any seeds intended for planting purposes, as they may have been sprayed with poisons. Also, do not eat potato sprouts, as they are toxic.

To sprout, you need a wide-mouthed glass jar, some netting (nylon, cheesecloth, or gauze), and a rubber band. Place a small amount (½ to 1 tablespoon) of the seeds or beans in the jar, fill the jar with lukewarm water, then place the netting over the mouth of the jar and secure with the rubber band. If you are using very small seeds, you might want to use two layers of netting so as not to lose any of the seeds in the rinsing process. Let the seeds soak overnight. In the morning, with the netting in place, drain the water out, then refill with fresh tap water, swirling it around to rinse the seeds. Drain this water out and allow the jar to drain inverted in the sink or in a dish drainer. Repeat the rinsings morning and evening for three to five days, depending upon the seeds or beans used.

Place sprouts in a plastic bag in the refrigerator to keep them fresh.

Seeds may be sprouted in light or in a dark cupboard, but never in direct sunlight as they dry out too quickly. Be sure to keep the seeds moist, because if they're too dry they won't develop properly. However, if they're too wet, they'll rot.

You can try sprouting combinations of seeds for salads, such as red clover, radish, and alfalfa; or use the bigger beans like mung, adzuki, and pea, marinated in your favorite dressing, as a crunchy salad on their own.

For more information on uses of sprouts or ways of sprouting, ask your local health-food store. They often have "starter kits" with samples of the various kinds of seeds and beans, netting, and full instructions on sprouting.

Dining Out

One of the most difficult problems confronting a vegetarian is finding a good meal away from home. Restaurants, airplanes—even your best friend's home—can be a minefield of problems in the battle to eat a meatless meal.

The best possible advice I can give you is to assert yourself. Don't let the waiter slip meat into your spaghetti sauce. Call the airlines in plenty of time to order a vegetarian meal. And don't let that friend sweet-talk you into trying her specialty of deep-fried hog knees.

Restaurants

The first rule of dining out for a vegetarian is to choose the restaurant wisely. If you walk into a place called "The Beef 'n Grog," you're in trouble. Seek out a restaurant that is likely to have not only vegetarian meals, but vegetarian meals with a little style.

The most obvious choice is a vegetarian restaurant or a

health-food bar. I highly recommend that you pick up a copy of *The Annual Directory of Vegetarian Restaurants,* compiled and edited by Loren Kennett Cronk (Daystar Publishing Company, P.O. Box 707, Angwin, CA 94508, $6.95). It lists restaurants all over the United States from Anchorage, Alaska, to Kennebunkport, Maine. And there's also an *International Directory* for you jet-setters.

The *Directory* lists everything from lunch counters in health-food stores to full-service restaurants with plenty of atmosphere to go with your quiche. It also tells you whether you can get vegan, lacto, and lacto-ovo dishes, and even indicates the purity of the ingredients. For example, do they use preservatives and artificial flavors? Restaurants that use organically grown foods are also pointed out. Finally, the book gives you directions to each place, plus how much you're likely to be charged for a meal. All in all, this is a pretty handy volume for a vegetarian on the move.

One other point about this book, however. It is not the definitive word. Although it has helped me numerous times to find a good restaurant, it couldn't possibly include every restaurant in every town; and it doesn't. I have favorite restaurants all over the world and not one of them is even mentioned in this book. But that's neither the fault of the restaurants nor the book. Because of the incredible growth in the number of vegetarian eateries in the last ten years, it's impossible to keep track of them all. So, if you've got time, do some exploring. It's half the fun.

If you can't find a vegetarian restaurant, the next logical place to find a good vegetarian meal is in a restaurant that serves ethnic foods. Italian, Chinese, Mexican, Middle Eastern, and Jewish restaurants are all good bets.

Any kind of cheese-stuffed pasta dish or spaghetti with marinara (meatless) sauce, plus a good salad and some of that delicious hot bread, make an Italian restaurant a great choice for a vegetarian. And don't forget fettucine, manicotti, eggplant Parmesan, and all those good anti-pastos.

Chinese restaurants are loaded with good stir-fried vegetable plates and mounds of hot steaming rice. There are mixed vegetables with almonds, bean cakes (tofu) in sweet and sour sauce, vegetable chop suey, and chow mein. One warning, however. Chinese restaurants often add heavy doses of MSG, or monosodium glutamate. Ask the waiter to hold the MSG and other salts.

Middle Eastern restaurants have a number of meatless dishes to choose from, including falafel, a vegetarian "meat" sandwich of deep-fried ground garbanzo beans topped with vegetables and a sesame sauce called tahini. And, of course, especially out West, there are Mexican restaurants that feature cheese enchiladas, bean and cheese burritos, beans and rice, and dozens of other meatless dishes. Other alternatives are Greek salads, and spinach or cheese pies. Finally, don't forget the Jewish delicatessen with kasha and potato knishes, bagels and cream cheese.

If you're stuck and can't find a good vegetarian restaurant or foreign-food place, there are ways to survive in your local coffee shop—sometimes quite well. You can always get a tossed salad, or cottage cheese and fresh fruits or vegetables, and many types of meatless sandwiches on wheat bread. Potato dishes of all types are usually on every local menu, but try to stick with a baked potato for health. Finally, don't forget cafeterias which offer a selection of vegetarian entrées and salads to choose from.

Handling Yourself in a Vegetarian Restaurant

More and more restaurants must realize there's a large segment of the population (estimates run as high as 10,000,000 Americans who are now vegetarians) who want some creativity and variety in a restaurant's meat-less dishes. And it's the responsibility of vegetarians to educate them.

A simple statement to your waiter can clear up a lot of problems. For example, just tell him, "We're vegetarians. Can you suggest something from your menu?" Or ask the chef. If there's a whole table of you, the chef is usually happy to oblige. In my experience, a good chef looks forward to coming out front and getting the customers' reactions.

Another effective technique is to get on a personal level with the maitre d' or the owner, if he's around. Like any other situation in life, if you make yourself known and liked as an individual, people will usually take care of you.

Also, don't be hesitant to ask a restaurant to prepare a vegetarian meal not on the menu. If you give them plenty of advance notice, they will often gladly oblige you.

Here are a few other hints for eating out. When order-ing a grilled-cheese sandwich or hashed browns, or any griddle-fried food, check to see if they are fried on the same griddle as the hamburgers, bacon, and other meats. This is particularly prevalent in short-order joints. When in doubt, simply order toasted sandwiches and baked po-tatoes. Another hint is to always ask if the vegetable soup is made with meat broth.

Finally, it's not a bad idea to carry a few supplemental items with you to the restaurant. A piece of fruit in a purse, herbal tea bags in your pocket, or a bag of raisins and nuts go a long way toward making a limited menu more enjoyable.

Dining at 40,000 Feet

When traveling by air, always call the airline a day or two in advance to order a vegetarian meal for your flight.

Order when you make a reservation or when you confirm. Many frequent travelers (both vegetarians and meat eaters), in fact, order special meals because they know the airline chefs take particular care in their preparation. And this special service is free.

When you get on board the plane, usually a flight attendant will simply call out your name and ask you to identify yourself. If something goes wrong and they serve you a regular meal, just remind them that you ordered a vegetarian meal. Most of the time they'll discover that the meal is on board.

Remember, too, that when traveling by air, you can always bring food with you. Pack a supply of herbal teas, fruits, sandwiches, nuts, and dried fruit.

One other important note. The loss of water from your system due to the dry and rapidly circulating air on planes is thought to be a major cause of jet-lag. So drink lots of water throughout a long flight, and watch out for beverages containing caffeine or alcohol, which dehydrate the body. The tiny cups and inconvenience of water fountains on airplanes does not make it easy to drink lots of water. So it's not a bad idea to bring along a plastic jug of your own water.

Part Six

VEGETARIANISM AND THE ATHLETE

The Vegetarian Athlete

I still remember vividly a scene at the 1980 Winter Olympics when ABC television commentator Jim McKay interviewed the coach of the Norwegian ski-jumping team which had just succeeded in capturing the most gold medals in their sport. McKay asked the coach why his team had abstained from eating meat for the previous year in preparation for the Olympics. In a moment of utter and beautiful simplicity, the coach answered, "Because it makes us jump farther."

The athlete and coach have for many years understood the importance of exercise for fitness. But now, more and more, they are becoming aware of diet as the other key factor in helping a body perform to its potential.

The old dietary clichés have died hard, however. Many athletes still believe that a big, lean, rare steak is the best preparation for battle. But it simply isn't true. More and more you see athletes preparing for competition by loading up with carbohydrates—in other words, grains and vegetables.

Although the vegetarian athlete labors in relative obscurity (most people in competing nations are meat-eaters), for the percentage of competitors who follow a vegetarian diet, the rate of success is remarkable. In fact, there is really little doubt that a vegetarian can compete with a meat-eater. Just look at a list of successful vegetarian athletes.

Olympic marathon winners who were vegetarians include Hannes Kolehmainen and El Ouafi, and an Olympic gold medal was taken in wrestling by S. V. Bacon, who also held the British National title in many weight divisions, including lightweight, welterweight, middleweight, and heavyweight. He held these last four titles into his forties. William Pickering swam the English Channel and broke the existing record while doing it. And Australian Alexander Anderson holds national records in weight lifting.

Perhaps the best-known vegetarian athlete, however, is Murray Rose, the swimming champion who became the youngest triple gold-medal winner by winning the 400- and 1500-meter freestyle and 1500-meter marathon events at the 1956 Olympics. Four years later at the 1960 Olympics, he became the first man in history to retain his 400-meter title. Later, he broke earlier records for the 400-meter and 1500-meter freestyle events, leaving his mark as one of the greatest swimmers of all time.

Personally, my athletic performance was dramatically improved by my vegetarian diet. And, of course, that improvement was graphically borne out by the scientific testing I underwent at the Percival Fitness Institute (See

Part I, The Vegetarian Fugitive). But these tests really only provided further proof of what I already knew, because the benefits I was receiving from my switch in diet were obvious.

Perhaps the most striking benefit was a more consistent level of energy and prolonged endurance. Having spent twenty-five years of my life as a meat-eater, I was constantly perplexed by the physical ups and downs that are a natural part of a high protein meat diet. But my energy level as a vegetarian has been so consistent that for me a low-energy day is indeed a rarity.

It takes about ten flights in a row, weird time schedules, plus an overload of work and tournament play to really exhaust me. But then one good night's sleep will revitalize me completely. I am still amazed to this day at the complete and rapid recovery I can make after exhausting myself.

Also, my energy level in a match is much more consistent. I can recover much faster from being completely out of breath. In fact, the testings at Percival's showed that my oxygen uptake increased 38 percent in one year. That means that simply by switching to a meatless diet, I was able to increase my lung capacity by at least one-third. This, coupled with a 50 percent increase in my blood flow, meant that I was able to get oxygen throughout my system at nearly double the rate of the previous year. And I improved these functions in the three succeeding years of testing.

Perhaps the greatest athletic advantage I got from my vegetarian diet was psychological. If you know you're healthy, if you know you can go all day, the prospect of fatigue never threatens you the way you know it threatens your opponent. If it's a tough match, I've got the energy to play tough. And I know it. Because my energy stays at a consistent level, I just don't suffer drastic mood swings or physical ups and downs.

How an Athlete Gets
His Energy

Perhaps the single most significant requirement of an athlete is his need for energy—lots of energy! And energy in the human body is basically supplied by carbohydrates, fats, and proteins. To understand how to meet your particular energy needs, it's important to understand how energy is manufactured in the body, and to know which are the most efficient sources of energy.

The first source of energy that your muscles tap comes from adenosine triphosphate, ATP, which is a chemical substance made in the muscles almost exclusively by carbohydrates and fats. ATP is the fuel our systems use for strenuous exercise of short duration, because no oxygen is needed for its metabolism. This is called an anaerobic exercise. So you can run a fifty-yard dash all-out and not really take a breath.

If this rapid energy consumption lasts for more than a few brief moments, the muscles begin to burn phosphocreatine, PC, which can instantly regenerate ATP. But even your supplies of PC will only keep you going at top speed for a few extra minutes.

Then the body's second line of energy kicks in—glycogen. Glycogen is made by the body from sugar glucose, and stored in limited amounts in the liver and muscles. When the ATP and PC are depleted, glycogen is metabolized in the muscles to produce ATP. This is also an anaerobic reaction.

When your glycogen stores are depleted, the body taps into its third-line source of energy, which comes from the metabolism of stored carbohydrates and fats. (As long as carbohydrates and fats are available, protein is utilized in only minute amounts for energy production.) This supply can be almost unlimited, but that's not the problem. The metabolism of fats and carbohydrates is an aerobic reaction, which means it takes more time and lots of oxygen to produce this energy. Thus the week-end jock will huff and puff after only a few minutes of tough exercise because his body is not conditioned to take in the large sup-

plies of oxygen needed to metabolize these fats and carbohydrates for energy. After his stores of ATP and PC are shot, so is he.

Glucose, then, is really the principal food for our energy demands. ATP is the fuel burned by our muscles, and glucose is the source of ATP. And in turn, glucose is derived from digested carbohydrates.

Glucose is being continually carried along the bloodstream, principally to the brain and muscles, but it's also carried to the vital organs, such as the heart and kidneys, supplying the energy for your body's vital functions. This constant supply of glucose gives you the sharpened sense of awareness and quick reflexes necessary for competition. A low glucose level in the blood results in drowsiness, fatigue, and even depression, often referred to as "low blood sugar."

The better conditioned the athlete, the more efficient is his flow of glucose. And if the competitor is loaded with meat protein instead of carbohydrates (the source of glucose), his efficiency will be seriously hampered.

Carbohydrates or Protein for Energy?

Many athletes, in an effort to pump up muscle tissue and increase their strength, mistakenly go on high-protein diets. In the first place, a balanced diet supplies far more protein than you need for even the most demanding sport. And secondly, protein is the least efficient energy source. The digestion of excess protein actually requires about five times as much energy as the digestion of carbohydrates or fats. The amino acids that make up protein must be converted into carbohydrates and go through additional reactions before they can be utilized for energy. The by-products of this metabolism must then be eliminated by the kidneys.

162

A further drawback to excess protein consumption for an athlete is the dehydrating effects of a high-protein regimen, because the body demands much larger amounts of water to eliminate protein by-products than carbohydrate by-products. In general then, proteins are inefficient sources of energy and are used for energy by the body only when the more efficient sources, carbohydrates and fats, are not available.

Most sports nutritionists now state that if you plan to train seriously for competition, your carbohydrate consumption should exceed more than half your diet. And a balanced vegetarian diet usually consists of at least 60 percent complex carbohydrates.

One important point, however, that you should be aware of, is that carbohydrates cannot be stored in any significant amounts in the body. Only enough, in fact, for about twelve hours of very light activity. Heavy exercise can deplete your carbohydrate stores in a couple of hours. So eating large meals two or three times a day is not the best way to go about getting your most efficient source of energy. Eating small carbohydrate meals and snacks spread throughout the day usually works the best.

Carbohydrate Loading

A technique called "carbohydrate loading" is in widespread use among athletes today, particularly those engaging in endurance events. Carbohydrate loading means, as the term implies, loading up on carbohydrates so that the sources of glycogen supplies in your body are at a peak on the day of a competitive event.

This usually entails a two-phase program. Starting five or six days prior to competition, an athlete restricts his diet to mostly proteins and fats, while training long and hard. After two or three days he will begin to tire easily due to a depletion of glycogen in his muscles. He then begins to load up heavily on carbohydrates, starting three days before an event. In other words, he is packing his muscles and system with massive stores of glycogen, from which his body can draw during competition.

Before trying this technique, it is important to realize that it is primarily meant to be used for athletes participating in endurance events, such as the marathon. And it should probably be used only for important events, not as a regular training diet. Also, it is not recommended that athletes over forty try this diet.

Eating Before Competition

For eleven years my prematch meal has been spaghetti, because it is a source of carbohydrates. And this provides the long-term breakdown into energy-producing glycogen.

For me, the best time to eat this plate of spaghetti is about two hours before the match. Then I know that when the match starts, I'll have energy, and yet won't feel full and sluggish. Because metabolism rates vary, do some personal experimenting to determine your best pregame mealtime.

The Importance of Drinking Water

It is always a good rule to drink plenty of water, but this becomes even more important before and during athletic competition. Start drinking extra water a couple of days prior to the event. And during the event, make sure you drink plenty of water at frequent, regular intervals. This is important for replenishing the fluids that are essential for vigorous exercise.

Part Seven

VEGETARIAN RECIPES

Breakfast

GRANOLA

5 cups rolled oats
1 cup sunflower seeds
1 cup sliced or slivered almonds
1 cup shredded or chipped coconut (unsweetened)
½ cup wheat germ
½ cup sesame seeds
½ cup bran
½ cup soy flour
½ cup powdered milk
1 cup oil
1 cup honey
¾ cup raisins

Combine all but last 3 ingredients and mix well. Stir together the oil and honey, and add to dry ingredients. Mix well. Spread into lightly greased 13 x 19-inch pan. Bake at 350° for about 45 minutes, stirring every 10 minutes. Add

the raisins the last 5 minutes. Don't overcook. The cereal will be golden and still look a little "wet" when done. Store in airtight container. Serve with milk.
Approximately 3 quarts (or 12–13 cups)

BANANA PROTEIN DRINK

1 cup milk
¼ cup milk powder
1 banana
1 teaspoon cinnamon

Blend all ingredients in a blender.
Serves 1

BLUEBERRY PANCAKES

1 cup whole-wheat flour
2 teaspoons baking powder
¼ teaspoon salt
Egg substitute equivalent to 1 egg
2 tablespoons oil
1 tablespoon honey
1 cup buttermilk
½ cup blueberries

Combine dry ingredients in one container and wet ingredients (except blueberries) in another. Just before cooking, combine and mix well. Fold in the blueberries. Heat a lightly oiled griddle or frying pan over medium heat. To test the pan for proper heat, sprinkle with a few drops of water. If the water sputters around, the heat is correct. Drop 1 rounded tablespoon full of batter onto griddle at a time, leaving 2 to 3 inches between each. Turn pancakes when bubbles appear on top and the underside is golden brown. Cook other side until golden brown.

Approximately 1 dozen pancakes

RAISIN AND BRAN MUFFINS

1 cup whole-wheat flour
1 cup bran
¼ cup wheat germ
1 tablespoon baking powder
¼ teaspoon salt
¼ cup oil
¼ cup honey
Egg substitute equivalent to 1 egg
⅔ cup milk
⅓ cup raisins

Stir together dry ingredients and set aside. Stir well to combine the oil, honey, egg substitute, milk, and raisins. Add flour mixture, stirring only until combined. Spoon batter evenly into 12 muffin-tin cups. Bake in 400° oven about 15 minutes or until muffins are golden brown.

12 muffins

SWISS MUESLI

4 tablespoons rolled oats
4 tablespoons milk
1 apple, chopped
1 banana, mashed
2 tablespoons chopped nuts

Soak the oats in the milk for about 10 minutes. Mix in the other ingredients.

Variations: Oranges, grapes, and raisins are also good in muesli. You could also add the juice of ½ lemon, honey, or yogurt to taste.

Serves 2

ONE-SIDED BANANA FRENCH TOAST

2 tablespoons cashew nuts
½ cup water
2 bananas
¼ teaspoon vanilla
Dash cinnamon
Butter or oil
4 slices bread

Grind the cashews in a blender until they are almost a flour. Add the water. While blending, add the bananas, vanilla, and cinnamon. Pour into a bowl, and dip a bread slice into the mixture. While the bottom side is soaking up the mixture, butter, or lightly oil, the top side of the bread. Place the bread, buttered side down, onto a lightly greased cookie sheet. Repeat with other slices of bread. Bake in 400° oven until the top side is golden brown. Turn once. Top with maple syrup.
Batter for 4 slices of bread

BREAKFAST HOT CEREALS

There are a large variety of grains that can be made into hot cereals, like oats, millet, buckwheat, barley, rye, brown rice, cornmeal, and wheat berries. And also a variety of ingredients that can be added just before serving, like raisins, chopped dates, sliced bananas, raw grated apple, sliced peaches, berries, or chopped nuts. The following recipe uses millet and raisins.

HOT MILLET CEREAL

½ cup millet (whole, hulled)
1 cup water
½ cup milk
¾ cup raisins

Combine millet, water, and milk in a saucepan. Cover and bring to a boil. Lower heat and let stand for about 15 minutes. Add raisins, and continue cooking about 5 minutes, or until millet is fluffed and all liquid is absorbed. Serve with milk and honey, if desired.
Serves 4

Lunch

PIZZA FOR LUNCH

For a quick pizza, use whole-wheat pita bread as the crust. Count on one "pita pizza" per serving.

> *1 piece pita bread*
> *¼ cup tomato or spaghetti sauce*
> *⅓ cup grated cheese*

Spread sauce on pita bread, and put cheese evenly over the top. Add your choice of the following toppings: mashed tofu, mushrooms, green pepper, ripe olive slices, lightly steamed vegetables. Put pizza on a cookie sheet and bake in 425° oven until the cheese is melted.

Variation: *Eggplant Pizza:* Slice an eggplant thin and place slices flat in a baking dish. Top with tomato sauce, oregano, and cheese. Bake in a 350° oven for about 20 minutes.

Serves 1

SUNFLOWER BURGERS

1 cup ground sunflower seeds
¼ cup ground peanuts
½ cup shredded carrot
½ cup minced celery
1 tablespoon oil
¼ cup tomato sauce or juice, or vegetable cocktail
Herb seasoning to taste

Combine ingredients and mix well. Make patties and place on a lightly greased cookie sheet. Bake at 350°, turning to brown on both sides. If desired, top with melted cheese.
Makes about 8 patties. Serves 3–4

SANDWICHES

Try for variety in your sandwiches, not just in the fillings, but also in the bread and the garnishes.

Bread: Put the filling on whole-wheat, rye, raisin, pumpernickel, or other nutritious breads. Or stuff the filling into pita (pocket) bread or roll it in chapatis.

Garnishes: Choose from different kinds of lettuce, shredded cabbage, watercress, fresh spinach, alfalfa sprouts, bean sprouts, cucumbers, tomatoes, chopped celery, sunflower or pumpkin seeds, or chopped nuts.

Fillings: Peanut butter (or other nut butter) with honey,
dates, raisins, granola, or bananas
- nut loaf with lettuce and mayonnaise
- avocado with mushrooms, cheese, and sprouts
- cream cheese with olives, or with apples
- bean spread with garnishes

MYSTERY SANDWICH SPREAD

This really is no mystery—it's a bean spread made of
either garbanzo beans or soybeans. But people just don't
seem excited to try a "bean spread." It is nutritious, tastes
good, and will have the consistency of a chicken- or tuna-
salad sandwich spread.

> *1 cup garbanzo beans or soybeans, cooked until
>   soft*
> *2 tablespoons mayonnaise*
> *1 cup chopped celery, or grated carrot, or both*
> *Dash tamari*
> *Herb seasoning*
> *1 tablespoon sweet pickle relish (optional)*

Mash the beans, either in a food processor, with a potato
masher, or with a fork. To do this in a blender, you may
need to add a little water. Then add the other ingredients
until you get the taste and texture you want. Experiment.
You can get delicious results.
Makes about 8 sandwiches

OPEN-FACED BROILED SANDWICHES

Assemble ingredients on toast, then broil in the oven until
cheese melts. Choose from the following combinations:

- lightly sautéed vegetables (like chopped eggplant, zucchini, or broccoli), sprinkled with oregano or basil, topped with tomato slices and grated cheese
- lightly sautéed and drained mushrooms, topped with grated cheese
- thin-sliced apples topped with grated cheese

OTHER LUNCH SUGGESTIONS

Consider some of the following as additions to your lunch.

- hot or cold soups
- yogurt mixed with fruit and nuts
- fresh fruit pieces or fruit salad
- crackers and cheese
- fresh vegetable salad
- raw vegetables with "dips"
- cottage cheese or bean spreads on lettuce

BEVERAGES

Don't forget variety in what you drink at lunch as well. Choose from milk, hot or cold carob drinks, fruit or vegetable juices, hot cider or herbal teas either on their own or in combination with juice. Combine fizzy mineral water or soda water with fruit juice for healthy soda. You can make orange juice frothy and delicious by adding ¼ cup milk powder to 1 cup of juice in a blender. Or try any combination of fruits and juice in a "smoothie."

BASIC SMOOTHIE

1 banana
Fruit (choose juicy fruits like papayas, mangoes,
oranges, or berries)
1 cup fruit juice
Honey or soft dates to taste
½ to 1 cup yogurt (optional)
Ice

Blend all ingredients in blender.
Serves 2

Soups

VEGETABLE STOCK

A few tips about making your own vegetable stock:

- Save the water used for steaming vegetables.
- Save vegetable scraps like outer leaves, stalks, and skins.
- Vegetable bouillon cubes are available and are convenient to use. You may want to add cubes to your own homemade stock. Or try some miso or tamari to flavor the broth.

To make the broth:
Chop up the scraps and put them in a large pot. Use the saved vegetable-steaming liquid, plus enough water to cover all the vegetables in the pot. Add some herbs like basil, oregano, thyme, or savory. Cover and simmer for about 30 minutes. Cool and strain, preserving the liquid. The stock can be stored in the fridge or the freezer in smaller containers.

SOUP GARNISHES

Try a variety of garnishes, like grated cheese, whole-wheat croutons, wheat germ, or a dab of yogurt or sour cream, topped with toasted almonds or seeds.

MINESTRONE SOUP

1 cup garbanzo beans
1 carrot, sliced
2 stalks celery, sliced
2 potatoes, peeled and cubed
5 to 6 ripe tomatoes, cut into chunks
ANY OR ALL OF THE FOLLOWING:
1 zucchini, sliced
1 cup cut-up string beans
1 cup chopped spinach
½ cup uncooked macaroni
1 cup chopped cabbage
2 teaspoons basil
1 teaspoon oregano
Chopped parsley
Grated Parmesan cheese

Wash garbanzo beans and soak overnight in 4 cups of water. Cook next day in soaking water. You may need to add more water, if so, use vegetable stock if possible. When beans are tender, add all other ingredients and simmer for about 1 hour. Serve with Parmesan cheese. Serves 6 to 8
Note: If you have cooked your beans previously and don't have the cooking water, use about 6 cups of vegetable stock to start the soup.

POTATO SOUP

3 medium-size potatoes
1 stalk celery
2 carrots
2 to 3 cups vegetable stock
½ cup chopped broccoli
1 cup milk
Salt and pepper

Chop potatoes, celery, and carrots and sauté for about 5 minutes. Add vegetable stock. Cook until vegetables are tender, about 15 to 20 minutes. Add broccoli just before the other vegetables are tender. Purée the soup in the blender. Add milk until the soup has the desired thickness. Add salt and pepper to taste.
Serves 4

QUICK CREAM OF SPINACH SOUP

1 package frozen spinach
3 tablespoons butter or oil
2 tablespoons flour
1 teaspoon salt
3 cups vegetable stock
1 cup light cream
Dash nutmeg

Cook spinach in ½ cup water and purée in a blender. Heat the butter or oil in a pot, mix in the flour and salt, and add the stock gradually, stirring steadily. Then add the spinach and cook for about 5 minutes. Stir in the cream and serve hot.
Serves 4 to 6

LENTIL SOUP

1 ½ cups lentils
1 ½ quarts stock
1 ½ cups chopped tomatoes
2 celery stalks and leaves, chopped
1 carrot, grated
1 tablespoon lemon juice
1 tablespoon molasses (optional)
Tarragon, thyme, basil, oregano (optional)

Simmer lentils in stock until tender, approximately 2 hours. Add the other ingredients and simmer until vegetables are tender.
Serves 6

CREAM OF BROCCOLI SOUP

2 tablespoons oil
3 to 4 cups chopped broccoli
2 tablespoons whole-wheat flour
3 cups vegetable stock
½ teaspoon salt
Dash tamari
Dash basil or thyme
1 cup milk (or ½ cup milk and ½ cup yogurt or sour cream)

Lightly sauté the broccoli in the oil in a pot. Add flour and mix. Add stock, salt, tamari, and herbs. Cook until broccoli is tender, about 5 to 10 minutes. Purée in the blender. Return to the pot, add milk and slowly reheat.
Serves 4 to 6

CREAM OF TOMATO WITH BARLEY SOUP

½ cup uncooked barley
1 tablespoon oil
1 cup sliced celery
2 tablespoons whole-wheat flour
5 cups chopped tomatoes
1 tablespoon honey
1 teaspoon basil
1 teaspoon oregano
3 cups vegetable stock
3 cups milk

Cook barley in 1½ cups water until done, about 45 minutes. While the barley is cooking, heat oil in a large pot and sauté the celery. Add flour and mix. Add all other ingredients except milk. Simmer for about 1 hour. Purée in a blender. Add milk and barley and slowly reheat.
Serves 6

CHILLED FRUIT SOUP

The following is just a guideline. The proportions of the ingredients will depend on the type of fruits you choose, and the consistency you desire.

2 cups fresh fruit
2 cups unsweetened fruit juice
½ cup cream or yogurt or nutmilk (like coconut)
½ apple, peeled and chopped (optional)
½ banana (optional)
Honey or dates to sweeten (optional)

Blend all ingredients in a blender. Chill. You can top with a sprig of fresh mint, sliced toasted almonds, or grated coconut.

Homemade Bread and Pastry

GREAT BREAD

6 cups warm water
2 tablespoons yeast
1 tablespoon salt
1 cup oil
1 cup honey
1 cup soy flour
3 cups oats
½ cup wheat germ
About 10 cups whole-wheat flour
About 4 cups unbleached white flour

In a large mixing bowl, dissolve yeast in warm water. Mix in all ingredients except unbleached flour. Mix in enough unbleached flour to make dough easy to handle and so that it starts to leave the sides of the bowl.

Turn dough onto lightly floured counter. Rub flour on your hands as well. Knead the dough until it is smooth and elastic. If dough becomes sticky, flour hands and surfaces, and continue adding just enough flour to the dough to prevent it from sticking. Kneading will take about 5 minutes.

Place dough in a large greased bowl, turning so the top is also greased. Cover with a clean cloth, place in a warm place, and let rise until double in size (about 1 hour).

Punch dough down, place it again on counter, knead lightly and divide into 6 parts. With fingers, smooth each portion of dough out into a rectangle about the width of your bread pan. Roll rectangle up like a jelly roll. Seal sides under and place, seam side down, into a greased loaf pan. Let rise again, about 30 minutes.

Bake at 400° for about 10 minutes, then turn oven down to 325° and bake for another 45 minutes, until bread is deep golden brown and sounds hollow when tapped. When bread is cooled, wrap it securely. It can be frozen if it is not all for immediate use.

6 loaves

Note: If you are making several loaves at a time, you may want to purchase some small reusable foil loaf pans. Or experiment with different shapes and containers.

QUICK WHOLE-WHEAT YEAST DOUGH

1½ tablespoons yeast
1½ cups lukewarm water
1½ tablespoons oil
¼ cup honey
1 teaspoon salt
3 cups whole-wheat flour

Dissolve yeast in warm water. Add all other ingredients and mix well. Turn dough onto floured counter and knead to a firm ball (about 3 minutes). Form into desired shape.

If making bread, shape into a loaf and put in an oiled bread pan. Place in an oven, turned to the warm setting, for about 10 minutes. Then turn heat to 400° and bake for about 20 minutes, or until brown and hollow-sounding when tapped.

This dough can also be used for delicious crescent rolls. On a well-oiled counter, roll dough into a circle about ¼ inch thick. Spread with soft butter. Cut into pie-shaped pieces and, beginning at round edge, roll up. Place on greased cookie sheet, point underneath. Bake at 375° for 15 minutes.

WHOLE-WHEAT PIE CRUST

2 cups whole-wheat flour, or whole-wheat pastry flour
¼ teaspoon salt
½ teaspoon baking powder
½ cup oil, or softened butter or margarine
4 tablespoons ice-cold water

Start out with cold utensils and ingredients. Mix flour, salt, and baking powder together in a bowl. Add the oil and mix with fork, or rub between hands until the mixture is crumbly. Add water, 1 tablespoon at a time, mixing lightly with a fork. Divide the dough into 2 balls. Roll the first ball out between two sheets of wax paper, or two opened plastic bags, until it is the right size for your pie plate. Peel off one side of wax paper and flip crust into pie plate, paper side up. Mold into the corners and remove second sheet of paper. Trim around the outside edges of the pie plate with a knife. Add filling. Put on top crust, and crimp together the edges of top and bottom crust with fork.

Makes 1 double pie crust

VOL-AU-VENT or PASTRY SHELLS

Follow above instructions, until dough is ready to be divided and rolled out. Roll out the dough until it is about ⅛ inch thick. Find the lid of a jar, or even a saucer, that is about 4 to 6 inches wide. Place it on the dough and cut around it with a knife. Take a muffin tin and turn it upside down. Drape the circles of dough over the cups of the muffin tin. Pleat the dough around the cup. Use alternate ones so they don't overlap. Prick bottoms, and bake at 450° for about 6 to 7 minutes.

Makes about 12 shells

Salads

To prepare salads, use as wide a variety of fresh fruits and vegetables as are available to you. Because improvisation is part of salad-making, it is difficult to set down recipes. What follows is intended only to encourage your own experimentation.

Tossed Green Salads

Leafy greens form the basis of a tossed salad. Use fresh, crisp greens and try combinations of head lettuce, leaf lettuce, tender spinach leaves, and leaves from other vegetables. Wash the greens carefully in cold water and dry well. Use whole, or tear with hands. Other salad ingredients could include: celery, carrots, raw cauliflower, broccoli, grated raw beets, tomatoes, fresh sweet corn or green peas, asparagus tips, bell peppers, zucchini, radishes, cucumber, sprouts, olives, cooked garbanzo beans, roasted soybeans, sunflower or pumpkin seeds, nuts, avocado, kelp or dulse, cheese, or a sprinkling of wheat germ. Herbs could include: basil, thyme, rosemary, oregano, or tarragon.

To assemble: Mix together greens and firm vegetables. If using oil and vinegar as dressing, add about 3 to 4 tablespoons oil and toss until all greens are coated. Add herbs sparingly and toss again.

Add about 2 tablespoons vinegar or lemon juice, or a combination of the two. Toss well. Now add grated vegetables, tomatoes, and garnishes like sprouts, seeds, croutons, etc. Serve cold.

BASIC SALAD DRESSING

A basic oil and vinegar or French dressing is made of about two parts oil to one part vinegar or lemon juice.

1 cup oil
¼ cup vinegar
¼ cup lemon juice
½ teaspoon dry mustard

Shake all ingredients together in a jar with a tight lid and refrigerate.

Variation: *Avocado Dressing:* Blend in soft avocado until desired consistency is reached.

EGGLESS MAYONNAISE

1 cup soy milk* or evaporated milk
1 cup oil (soybean oil is good)
½ teaspoon salt
2 teaspoons honey
¼ cup lemon juice

Put milk in blender. With blender on, add oil slowly until mixture thickens. Add salt, honey, and lemon juice. Mix well.
*If you don't have fresh soy milk and are using packaged soy milk powder such as Soyagen or Soyamel, omit the honey and increase the lemon juice to ⅓ cup. Mix powdered soy milk and water first in blender.

CABBAGE SALAD

3 cups shredded or chopped cabbage
1 carrot, grated
1 stalk celery, chopped
Mayonnaise, or a combination of sour cream and
    mayonnaise
Seasoning salt

Toss all ingredients together, adding the mayonnaise to desired taste and consistency.
Serves 4

FRUIT SALADS

Use whatever fruits are in season or reasonable to purchase. Choose from oranges, grapefruits, melons, pineapples, peaches, plums, apples, pears, cherries, berries, bananas, mangoes, papayas, and dried fruits like raisins.

A few tips for making fruit salads:
- Cut fruits into bite-size chunks.
- When peeling and cutting juicy fruits like oranges, grapefruits, and pineapples, make sure all the juice gets into the salad.
- When cutting apples and pears, sprinkle or brush them with a little lemon juice so they don't turn brown.
- Bananas can also be brushed with lemon. Don't go overboard on bananas, as their flavor is a dominant one.

WALDORF SALAD

2 apples, cut into chunks
1 stalk celery, chopped
⅓ to ½ cup chopped nuts (walnuts, pecans, cashews)
⅓ to ½ cup raisins
½ cup cubed cheese (mild Cheddar or cream cheese—optional)
Mayonnaise, yogurt, or sour cream

Combine all ingredients, and moisten to taste with mayonnaise, yogurt, or sour cream, or a combination. You could also add a little lemon juice and honey to the dressing if you wished.
Serves 4

Dinner

The following recipes are designed to be the entrée, or main dish for your dinner. Obviously dinner can be as simple as homemade bread and hearty soup, or as light as a salad. However, many new vegetarians are often at a loss to know how to prepare a main meal without just making several "side" dishes of vegetables. Even at the best restaurants, when the chef hears you are a vegetarian, he will prepare you a platter of cooked vegetables. Just let these recipes be an introduction to the wide variety of entrées that can be at the center of a vegetarian meal.

SPINACH LASAGNE

*2 bunches spinach, chopped, or 1 package frozen
    chopped spinach*
*½ pound cooked lasagna noodles (whole-wheat or
    spinach noodles are good)*

¼ pound mushrooms, sliced
1 tablespoon oil
4 cups favorite tomato sauce, or 2 15-ounce cans
* or jars of sauce*
¾ cup cottage cheese or ricotta
¾ pound mozzarella cheese

Steam fresh spinach until tender, or defrost frozen spinach until it can be broken apart. Cook lasagna noodles until tender, and drain. Brown mushrooms in oil, and add tomato sauce. (If adding spices to canned sauce, let this simmer.) In a large roasting pan or casserole, arrange in layers: lasagna noodles, spinach, cottage cheese, and mozzarella. Cover with tomato sauce and mushrooms, seeing that the sauce also covers the sides of the casserole. Bake at 375° for 45 minutes.

Variation: *Lasagna Pinwheels:* Reduce amount of cheese to about ¼ to ⅓ pound and shred it. Mix together the spinach, cottage cheese, and mozzarella. Spread out each noodle and put about 3 tablespoons of the mixture all along its length. Roll up the noodle and place it in the baking pan so you can see the design. Continue until you have rolled all noodles. (Any leftover filling may be mixed with the sauce.) Reduce sauce to about 2 cups and pour over top of noodles. Reduce baking time to about 20 to 30 minutes.

Serves 6

MUSHROOM CALZONE

Calzone is kind of a pizza turnover. When considering preparation time, don't forget to include time for dough to rise.

Dough:
1 tablespoon yeast
1 cup warm water
3 tablespoons oil or melted butter
2 tablespoons honey
3 cups flour (whole-wheat, or mixture of whole-wheat and unbleached white flour)

Dissolve yeast in water and add other ingredients. Knead for about 5 minutes. Cover and set in a warm place to rise for about 1 hour. Punch down and turn out onto floured counter. Divide into six equal portions. Roll out each portion into a circle about ¼ inch thick. For each, use one-sixth of the filling, placing the filling over one-half of the circle. Leave a ½-inch rim. Fold the empty side over the filling, and moisten and press edges together to seal. Prick in a few places with a fork. Bake on an oiled tray in a preheated 450° oven for about 15 to 20 minutes, or until golden brown. Brush with melted butter.

Filling:
1 tablespoon oil
½ cup chopped celery
½ pound mushrooms, sliced
½ cup sliced black olives
½ cup chopped tomatoes
2 tablespoons tomato paste
1 teaspoon basil

1 teaspoon oregano
2 cups grated mozzarella cheese
½ cup grated Parmesan cheese

Put a little oil in a heated frying pan. Sauté the celery and mushrooms. Add all other ingredients to the pan, except the cheeses. Simmer, covered, for about 15 minutes. Remove from heat and allow to cool a bit. Mix in cheese. Serves 6

NUT LOAF

2 tablespoons butter or oil
2 stalks celery, chopped
1 carrot, grated
1 cup chopped walnuts
1 cup chopped cashews
½ cup ground peanuts
¼ cup ground sunflower seeds
½ cup rolled oats
1 pound cottage cheese
1 block tofu, well drained and mashed
½ teaspoon basil
½ teaspoon oregano
Egg substitute to equal 2 eggs

Lightly sauté the celery in the butter or oil. Mix all ingredients together. Put into a greased 5″ x 9″ loaf pan and bake for approximately 1½ hours at 375°. Serve hot with gravy or mushroom sauce. Leftovers are great in sandwiches. Serves 4–6

VEGETABLE STEW

2 tablespoons butter or oil
2 carrots, sliced
3 stalks celery, sliced
2 potatoes, sliced
2 tomatoes, cut into chunks
1 cup corn kernels
1 cup peas
2 vegetable bouillon cubes
2 teaspoons arrowroot
Herbs to taste (Spike*, dill weed, oregano, basil)

In pot over medium heat, melt butter and lightly sauté carrots and celery. Add potatoes, tomatoes, corn, and peas to pot. Dissolve bouillon cubes and arrowroot in 1½ cups water, and add to pot. Stir in herbs. Lower heat, cover, and simmer for about ½ hour. Serve over brown rice.

Variation: Tofu is delicious when added to this stew, because it picks up the flavor of the broth and spices. Use ½ block (about 1 cup) of tofu, cut into 1-inch cubes. Especially good if deep-fried first.

To deep-fry tofu, arrange the cubes on a doubled cloth towel. Top with another doubled towel, pat down firmly and let stand for about half an hour. Heat oil in a wok, pot, or deep-fryer to 350°. Place the tofu in the oil and deep-fry until golden brown. Drain on absorbent towel. Serves 4–6

* A commercially available seasoning that contains several different herbs and spices.

CHILI

2 cups raw kidney beans
2 stalks celery, chopped
1 small green pepper, chopped
1 carrot, chopped
2 to 3 tablespoons oil
2 cups chopped tomatoes
2 tablespoons tomato paste
1 tablespoon lemon juice
1 teaspoon each basil, cumin, oregano
1 to 2 teaspoons chili powder
¾ cup chopped cashews
Grated cheese, preferably Cheddar

Soak beans in 6 cups water overnight. If possible, use vegetable stock instead of water, or add a vegetable bouillon cube to the soaking water. Simmer in soaking water until tender, about 2 hours. Sauté celery, green pepper, and carrot in the oil until tender. Add to beans. Add all other ingredients, except cashews, to the beans and heat. If too dry, add a little tomato sauce or tomato juice. Taste for seasoning. Before serving, add cashews, and top with grated cheese.
Serves 6 to 8

TOFU CABBAGE CASSEROLE

3–4 tablespoons oil
1 small head cabbage, shredded
1 small zucchini, grated
2 medium carrots, grated
½ block tofu (about 1 cup), drained and cut into
*   1-inch pieces*
1½ cups grated cheese (combination of moz-
*   zarella, Monterey jack, and Parmesan)*
½ cup sliced almonds

Heat oil in a pan. Sauté cabbage, zucchini, and carrots until tender. Add the tofu. Remove from heat when the tofu is hot. In a baking dish, layer half the cabbage mixture, then half the cheese, then remaining cabbage mixture and cheese. Top with almonds. Bake uncovered at 350° for about 20 minutes, until the almonds are lightly browned.
Serves 6

WALNUT AND CELERY CASSEROLE

1 cup chopped walnuts
1 cup chopped celery
1 cup grated Cheddar cheese
1 cup cooked brown rice
Seasoning to taste

Place all ingredients in a baking dish in 350° oven for about 20 minutes, until cheese is melted.
Serves 4

MUSHROOM STUFFED CABBAGE

1 head cabbage
2 tablespoons oil
½ pound mushrooms, sliced
½ cup chopped celery
¼ cup cooked brown rice
Salt, pepper, Spike seasoning to taste (see p. 194)
2 cups favorite tomato sauce, or 1 15-ounce can sauce

Briefly steam the head of cabbage (about 5 minutes). Carefully remove 16 leaves. Chop up 2 cups of the remaining cabbage and spread in the bottom of a casserole.

Heat oil in a pan and sauté mushrooms and celery. Remove from heat and add in the cooked rice and seasonings. Place 1 to 2 tablespoons of the mixture on each cabbage leaf and roll up. Place each roll, folded side down, over the shredded cabbage in the casserole. Add tomato sauce. Cover and bake for about 45 minutes at 350°. Remove cover for last 10 minutes.
Serves 4

CHEESE FONDUE

½ to ¾ pound cheese, grated (any combinations of Swiss, Cheddar, Monterey jack, Gruyère, Emmenthal)
4 ounces cream cheese (optional)
1½ tablespoons arrowroot
⅛ teaspoon each dry mustard, salt, nutmeg, pepper
1 tablespoon honey or to taste (optional)
1 cup buttermilk
Cubes of French bread

Mix the cheese with the arrowroot in the fondu pot. Over medium heat on the stove, add all other ingredients. Stir constantly until the cheese has melted and the mixture is completely smooth. (Try using a wire whisk.) If the fondue is not thick enough, add a little more cheese. Season to taste. When it is bubbling, put it over the fondue burner. The fondue should be simmering gently. Dip cubes of French bread into this with fondue forks. You can also try dipping a few raw or lightly steamed vegetables.
Serves 4

ENCHILADAS

Light oil for frying
12 corn tortillas
Filling:
6 ounces (about 1½ cups) grated Cheddar cheese
6 ounces (about 1½ cups) grated Monterey jack cheese
1 can pitted black olives, sliced
1 cup sour cream (optional)

Set aside about 1 cup of the grated cheese. Mix together all other ingredients.

ENCHILADA SAUCE*

*1 small green chili pepper, minced, or chili pow-
der to taste
½ teaspoon each cumin, oregano, salt
2 tablespoons oil
½ cup chopped celery
3 cups tomato purée*

Sauté chili and spices in oil. Add celery and tomato purée
and simmer about ½ hour, stirring often. Put in a flat
bowl or pan.

To assemble enchiladas:
Heat about ¼ inch of oil in a frying pan. Fry each tortilla
on both sides just long enough to soften (only about 10
seconds per side). Drain on paper towel. Dip each tortilla
into the enchilada sauce. Place about ¼ cup of filling in a
fat line on each tortilla and roll up. Arrange in a baking
dish. Cover with remaining sauce, and top with reserved
cheese. Bake uncovered in a 350° oven about 20 minutes.
Serves 6

Variation: *Stacked Enchiladas:* Instead of rolling the enchiladas, stack them flat on top of each other. After dipping each tortilla in oil and sauce, place in a casserole
dish. Sprinkle about ¼ cup filling over the flat tortilla.
Add remaining tortillas, prepared the same way. Pour remaining sauce over the top and bake uncovered for about
15 minutes in a 350° oven.

* Enchilada sauce can be purchased, if you wish. It can be mixed
with tomato sauce if you find it too spicy. For 12 enchiladas, you will
need about 2 cups of sauce.

TOSTADAS

A tostada is an open-faced sandwich with a whole, crisp tortilla as the bottom layer. Usually, count on 1 tostada per person.

Heat about ½ inch oil in a frying pan and fry tortillas until golden brown and crisp.

The next 2 layers are:

Refried beans (¼ to ½ cup per tostada)
Grated cheese (about ⅓ cup per tostada)

Choose from the following for the other layers:

Chopped tomatoes
Sliced avocado or guacamole
Sliced olives
Sprouts
Garnishes of sour cream and tomato sauce

Pile on the beans, cheese, and all other ingredients. Pick it up in your hands and enjoy it.

REFRIED BEANS

2 cups dry pinto beans, washed and cleaned
6 cups water
½ cup oil

Simmer pinto beans in the water in a covered pot until they are very soft, about 2 to 3 hours. Mash beans and add oil. Mix well and continue stirring until beans are thickened.

200

Variation: Sauté green pepper, celery, chopped tomatoes, salt, and cumin to taste, and add to the beans. When ready to serve, add grated cheese on top.

COUNTRY VEGETABLE PIE

Unbaked pastry for 2-crust 9-inch pie
1 cup chopped broccoli
1 cup chopped cauliflower
½ cup corn
½ cup peas
½ cup chopped tomatoes
½ cup mushrooms
1½ cups white sauce (see recipe page 212)
1½ cups grated cheese
Oregano, salt to taste

Mix all ingredients together. (Obviously you can choose any of your favorite vegetables for this pie.) Put into a 9-inch pastry-lined pie pan. Adjust top crust. Prick the top with a fork and bake for about 45 minutes to 1 hour in a 350° oven.
Serves 4

FLAKY BROCCOLI STRUDEL

½ pound filo dough leaves (about 10 leaves)
(These can be purchased, usually frozen in 1-pound packages. For this recipe, you will need only half the package, so rewrap the remainder and refreeze.)
¼ pound butter (or combination of butter and oil)

Filling:

Prepare the following filling first:

5 cups chopped raw broccoli
1 cup chopped celery
¼ pound mushrooms, sliced
2 cups bread crumbs
2 cups grated cheese
Oil for frying
1 lemon

Sauté the broccoli, celery, and mushrooms in oil for about 4 to 5 minutes, until tender. Put in large bowl and add bread crumbs and cheese. Cut lemon in half and squeeze juice over the mixture.

To assemble the strudel:

- It is helpful to have a pastry brush, wax paper to work on, and a slightly damp towel to place over filo leaves so they won't dry out. You will be assembling 2 strudels, using 5 filo leaves for each.
- Melt the butter. Lay out 1 filo leaf and brush the melted butter over it. Lay next leaf on top and brush butter on it. Repeat until you have layered and buttered all 5 leaves.
- Spread half the filling across the bottom third of the pile, leaving about 2 inches free at bottom and sides. Fold over edges at left and right sides. Roll the strudel forward like a jelly roll.
- Carefully lift the strudel and put it seam side down on an oiled cookie sheet. Brush top with melted butter. Make three or four diagonal slashes through the crust to the filling.
- Repeat process with the second strudel.
- Bake about 30 minutes at 375°, until golden and crisp.

Serves 4 to 6

Note: This recipe is actually fairly simple to make, and there are diagrams for assembling a strudel on the filo package. It just takes about as long to describe the process as it does to do it.

9.5 CREPES

When we were experimenting with different fillings and sauces for these crepes, we were rating the combinations from 1 to 10. This one was a strong 9.5!

Crepes:
1 cup whole-wheat flour
½ cup unbleached white flour
2½ cups milk
4 tablespoons butter, oil, or margarine
1½ tablespoons arrowroot

Blend all ingredients in a blender. Refrigerate for about ½ hour, and then whisk together.

Heat small nonstick skillet on medium-high flame. (Nonstick pans really ease crepe-making. If you don't have one, brush small pan lightly with melted butter or a few drops of oil.) When pan is hot, pour in enough batter to coat bottom of pan, and a little up the sides.

Pour excess batter back into bowl and note correct amount. This will probably be about ⅛ to ¼ cup of batter per crepe. (As you pour the batter into the pan, tilt pan in all directions with other hand, so the batter will completely cover the bottom.) The crepe should be as thin as possible.

Cook about 1 minute, until underside is lightly browned. Flip it onto the other side, using a spatula, and cook about 30 seconds, or until lightly browned. Slide the crepe onto a clean towel, and repeat with remaining batter.

Filling:

8 ounces cream cheese, softened
¾ to 1 cup cheese sauce (below)
1 package frozen spinach, cooked
8 ounces mushrooms, sliced
2 tablespoons butter or oil
Salt, pepper to taste

In a mixing bowl, beat the cream cheese with about 1 cup of the cheese sauce. Add the spinach and mix well. Sauté the mushrooms in the butter or oil, and add them to the mixture. Season to taste.

Cheese sauce:

4 tablespoons oil
4 tablespoons flour
2½ cups milk
2 cups grated cheese
½ teaspoon salt
¼ teaspoon dry mustard

Mix oil and flour in a saucepan until smooth. Stir in milk and bring to a boil. When smooth, reduce heat to simmer and stir in cheese and seasonings.

To assemble the crepes:

Place about ¼ to ⅓ cup of filling in the center of each crepe. Roll the crepe to enclose the filling, and place, seam side down, in a greased baking dish. Cover with foil. Make a few slits with a knife in the foil. Bake at 350° for about 15 minutes. Serve with remaining cheese sauce to pour over top.

Variations: You can fill crepes with any fresh, steamed, or sautéed vegteables, or leftovers. In the recipe above, you could omit the spinach or the mushrooms, or you could use a white sauce instead of a cheese sauce.

SPANISH TOWN BAKED AVOCADO

3–4 tablespoons oil
½ to 1 teaspoon freshly grated ginger
1 cup sliced carrots
1 cup chopped celery
1 cup chopped broccoli
1 cup chopped cauliflower
1 cup sliced mushrooms
1 cup chopped tomatoes
1 cup pecans
4 teaspoons honey
4 medium avocados, barely ripe

Heat oil in a frying pan, and put in the ginger. Then add the carrots, celery, broccoli, cauliflower, mushrooms, tomatoes, and pecans (in that order), and sauté until just tender. Drizzle the honey over during the last few minutes of cooking.

Cut the avocados in half and discard the pits. Scoop the avocados out of the shells (reserving the shells), in either small pieces or balls, and add them to the sautéed vegetables. Place the mixture in the empty avocado shells and bake at 350°, until the avocado is just heated through. This can be served with shredded coconut.
Serves 4

VOL-AU-VENT CREOLE WITH
AVOCADO SAUCE

Pastry shells for 4 to 6 people (see recipe page 185,
  or buy frozen patty shells or puff pastry shells.)
½ cup chopped celery
1 cup chopped cauliflower
1 cup chopped broccoli
1 cup sliced mushrooms
1 cup tomatoes, chopped to pulp
⅓ cup tomato juice
Seasoning to taste (salt, pepper, basil, oregano,
  thyme)
1 cup grated Cheddar cheese (optional)

Lightly sauté the celery, cauliflower, broccoli, and mushrooms. Then add tomatoes, juice, and seasoning, and
continue to heat until flavors have mingled, but vegetables are still crisp. Spoon into pastry shells. If desired, top
with grated cheese. Put in oven at 350° until shells are
heated. Serve with avocado sauce.

Variation: Before serving, put all ingredients into the
        avocado sauce and then spoon the mixture
        into heated pastry shells.

Serves 4–6

AVOCADO SAUCE

This sauce will only taste as delicious as the avocado
that's in it, so check the taste of the avocado first.

1 cup diced ripe avocado
2 cups cream
Dash lemon juice, salt, pepper, ginger

Sauté the avocado until soft. Add cream and seasonings. Boil the cream, stirring constantly, until it reaches the desired consistency.

WEST INDIAN RICE PATÉ WITH ALMOND SAUCE

2 cups cooked rice (for special occasions, try wild rice)
1½ cups whole-wheat bread crumbs
1 cup chopped nuts (walnuts, pecans)
1 cup chopped celery
1 cup chopped apples
¾ cup raisins
2 tablespoons honey
2 tablespoons oil
Egg substitute equivalent to 2 eggs

Mix all ingredients. Bake in oiled 5″ x 9″ loaf pan at 375° for about 1 hour, until firm. Serve with almond sauce. Serves 6

ALMOND SAUCE

⅓ to ½ cup almond paste (see recipe below)
2 cups cream
1 cup sliced almonds

In a saucepan over medium heat, combine the almond paste and the cream. Continue stirring until all paste has dissolved and cream is thickened. Add sliced almonds.

Almond paste:
½ cup whole blanched almonds
¼ cup honey
1 teaspoon almond extract

Grind almonds a few at a time in blender until consistency of flour. Work in honey and almond extract.
Notes: 1. It's the almond sauce that makes this dish so special, but it also makes for a rich, sweet entrée. Make your servings small and accompany with simple, fresh side dishes.
2. If you have any paste left over, heat it with cream and a little arrowroot to thicken, to make almond soup. Also delicious chilled.

ALMOND STIR-FRIED VEGETABLES WITH TOFU

1 block tofu, cut into 1-inch cubes
Whole blanched almonds
Chopped raw vegetables, any combination of the
*   following: carrots, peas, celery, cauliflower,*
*   green beans, broccoli, zucchini, snow peas,*
*   bamboo shoots, water chestnuts, mushrooms*
Oil
Tamari

Heat oil in a wok or heavy frying pan over medium-high heat. Lightly brown the tofu and almonds, remove with slotted spoon, and set aside. Put the vegetables that need longer cooking into the pan first, tossing them in the oil until they are coated. Stir-fry for about a minute, then add the vegetables that need less cooking time. Continue stirring for only a few more minutes, until the vegetables are almost crisp-tender. Add the tofu to the pan and sprinkle a little tamari sauce over the mixture. Remove from the heat, mix in the almonds, and serve immediately.

SWEET AND SOUR TOFU

Substitute any of the vegetables listed above for those in this recipe if desired.

4 tablespoons oil
1 cup celery, chopped on the diagonal
1 cup carrots, chopped on the diagonal
1 cup broccoli, cut into bite-size pieces
1 cup cauliflower, cut into bite-size pieces
2 cups tomato sauce
½ cup water
4 tablespoons honey
2 tablespoons lemon juice
1 block tofu, cut into 1-inch cubes

Sauté the vegetables in the oil until crisp-tender. Mix together the tomato sauce, water, honey, and lemon juice and add to the vegetables. Allow to simmer until the sauce has thickened. Add the tofu pieces, making sure they are well stirred into the sauce. Continue cooking until the tofu is heated. Serve over brown rice.
Serves 4

NOODLES AND VEGETABLES

Noodles (try Oriental chow mein noodles if available)

Chopped vegetables, any combination of the following: carrots, bell peppers, broccoli, tomatoes, potatoes, cauliflower, zucchini, mushrooms

Tamari

Grated Cheddar or Monterey jack cheese

Boil noodles in water. Meanwhile, fill a pan about one-quarter full of water, and insert vegetable steamer. First put in vegetables that need the most cooking, steam a little, then add the rest of the vegetables. Steam vegetables until just tender. Drain noodles, place in a serving bowl, add vegetables, sprinkle with tamari sauce, and top with grated cheese. Make sure vegetables are served immediately, so the cheese will melt.

Sauces

BROWN GRAVY

2 tablespoons whole-wheat flour
2 tablespoons oil
2 teaspoons tamari
1 cup vegetable broth (may be made with water
and broth seasoning)

Mix flour, oil, and tamari sauce over low flame. Stir vegetable broth into the mixture and continue stirring until gravy is smooth.
Note: A tip on making smooth gravies and sauces: Many a lumpy gravy has been saved thanks to a wire whisk. Invest in one to stir your sauces.

WHITE SAUCE

2 tablespoons butter or oil
2 tablespoons flour
1 cup milk
Dash of salt

Slowly melt the butter or heat the oil. Add flour, stirring until well mixed. Simmer for a couple of minutes. Slowly stir in the milk, and salt if desired. Continue simmering sauce, stirring often with a wire whisk, until the sauce is smooth and the desired consistency.

Variation: *Cheese sauce:* When white sauce is smooth and at a low boil, stir in 1 cup of grated cheese.

MUSHROOM SAUCE

2 cups sliced mushrooms
3 tablespoons butter or oil
3 tablespoons flour
1½ cups milk
Salt, pepper, tamari to taste

Fry mushrooms in butter or oil until soft. Add flour and stir to coat mushrooms. Stir in milk and seasonings to taste. Stir frequently over low heat until mixture thickens.

SWEET AND SOUR SAUCE

2 tablespoons oil
¼ teaspoon grated fresh ginger
1 cup pineapple chunks

1 cup pineapple juice, unsweetened
¼ cup honey
¼ cup lemon juice
2 tablespoons catsup
1 tablespoon tamari or soy sauce
1 tablespoon arrowroot

Heat the oil and add the fresh ginger and pineapple chunks. Add the remaining ingredients, except the arrowroot. Dissolve the arrowroot in 3 tablespoons water, then add to the sauce. Stir sauce until thickened to the desired consistency.

EASY FRESH TOMATO SAUCE

4 cups chopped tomatoes (about 6 to 8 tomatoes),
*   blended for several minutes in blender*
1 stalk celery, minced
½ bell pepper, minced
¼ teaspoon each oregano, basil, thyme
½ teaspoon salt
1 teaspoon honey

Simmer all ingredients together until flavors have blended.

SPAGHETTI SAUCE

This recipe is a good way to take the bite out of canned tomato sauce, and also to add a little crunch to it.

1 cup mixed vegetables
3 cups tomato sauce
Herbs (basil, rosemary, oregano, thyme, marjoram) to taste
Oil
1 tablespoon whole-wheat flour
½ cup cream or milk

Sauté vegetables until tender-crisp. Add tomato sauce and herbs and simmer covered for about 15 to 20 minutes. In a separate pan, heat ½ to 1 tablespoon oil and stir in the flour. Add the cream and stir until cream thickens. Add to tomato sauce.

Desserts

BANANA YOGURT PIE

Crust:
⅓ cup rolled oats
¼ cup chopped walnuts
¼ cup raisins
¼ cup chopped dates
2 tablespoons oil or melted butter

Mix all ingredients together. (Add a little water if needed for ingredients to stick together.) Press into a 9-inch pie plate. Bake about 10 minutes at 250°.

Filling:
⅔ cup yogurt
8 ounces cream cheese, softened
1 teaspoon vanilla
2 tablespoons honey
2 bananas, sliced
Shredded coconut

Beat together the yogurt, cream cheese, vanilla, and honey until smooth. Line bottom of pie shell with banana slices. Sprinkle with coconut. Pour yogurt mixture over top. Refrigerate several hours or overnight before serving. **Variation:** Use blueberries instead of bananas.

TOFU CHEESECAKE

Crust:
1 cup finely crushed graham crackers
¼ cup melted butter or margarine
1 tablespoon honey

Graham crackers can be crushed by putting them in a plastic bag and rolling with a rolling pin. Mix all ingredients together and press into the bottom of a 9-inch pie plate. Bake about 5 minutes in a 350° oven.

Filling:
2 cups drained and mashed tofu
2 bananas
2 tablespoons lemon juice
½ cup honey
2 teaspoons vanilla
1 cup crushed pineapple, drained

Combine all ingredients except pineapple and mix in blender until smooth. Fold in pineapple and pour into pie shell. Bake for about 45 minutes to 1 hour. Chill several hours, then spread on topping.

Topping:
*1 cup frozen strawberries (unsweetened), thawed
    and drained*
1 tablespoon honey
1 teaspoon arrowroot

Combine and cook until thickened. Spread on cheesecake and refrigerate.

CAROB FONDUE

¼ pound butter
⅜ cup honey
⅜ cup carob powder
¼ cup milk

In a fondue pot over burner, melt butter. Add honey and carob, and whisk together until smooth. Slowly add the milk until you have the taste and consistency desired. With fondue forks, dip any of the following into the carob fondue.

apples, cut into chunks and brushed with lemon
strawberries, washed and whole
banana, cut into chunks and brushed with lemon
pears, cut into chunks and brushed with lemon
Serves 4–6

LIGHT FRUIT FONDUE

If serving dessert fondues, it's nice to give a choice to people who wish a lighter, less sweet dessert.

1 16-ounce can peaches in unsweetened juice
1 teaspoon arrowroot
1 teaspoon vanilla

Blend ingredients in a blender until smooth. Pour into fondue pot and heat until bubbling and thickened. Dip in the fruits listed in Carob Fondue recipe.
Serves 4–6

APPLE TARTS

1 recipe pastry shells (see recipe page 185)
2 tablespoons butter
1 12-ounce can frozen apple juice, thawed
3 tablespoons tapioca
7 to 8 cups apples (about 7 or 8 apples), cored and sliced thin
1 teaspoon cinnamon
⅛ teaspoon salt

Simmer all ingredients, except pastry, until tender, about 15 minutes. Spoon about ⅓ cup filling into each tart. Tarts can be topped with whipped cream, sweetened with a dash of maple syrup, and sprinkled with chopped nuts. 1 dozen tarts

BANANA ICE CREAM

Freeze bananas, either in their skins or peeled, in plastic bags. Cut them in pieces and blend them a little at a time in a blender, just until smooth. Top with fruit or nuts. You can even make parfaits, layering the banana ice cream with other fruits, like berries (thawed and drained, if frozen), ripe papayas, mangoes, or peaches.

CAROB-COATED BANANAS

½ cup water
½ cup carob powder
⅓ cup honey
1 teaspoon vanilla
6 bananas, cut in thirds
Nuts, chopped

Mix all ingredients together in a saucepan, except bananas and nuts. Cook slowly until sauce reaches desired consistency. Dip bananas into carob sauce, then roll in chopped nuts. Stick toothpicks into bananas and freeze. Eat frozen.
Makes 18 pieces

FRUIT IN SOUR CREAM

1 cup seedless grapes
1 cup halved fresh strawberries
1 cup pineapple chunks
⅛ cup maple syrup
⅓ cup sour cream

Combine fruit. Stir maple syrup into sour cream. Keep everything chilled until ready to serve. Pile the sour cream onto the fruit and toss together.
Serves 4

CARROT CAKE

½ cup raisins
½ cup melted butter or oil
½ cup honey
1 teaspoon vanilla
Egg substitute equivalent to 1 egg
1 cup grated carrots
1 ¼ cups whole-wheat flour
2 teaspoons baking powder
½ teaspoon salt
½ teaspoon cinnamon
½ cup chopped walnuts

Mix together the raisins, butter, honey, vanilla, and egg substitute. In a separate bowl, mix together all the other ingredients. Then stir the dry ingredients into the wet ingredients. Pour into an oiled 8-inch baking pan, and bake at 350° for about 30 minutes. Cool, then remove from pan and apply frosting (see recipe below). If you wish to make a layer cake, then double the ingredients and bake in two pans.

FROSTING

4 ounces cream cheese, softened
¼ cup butter, softened
¼ cup honey
1 teaspoon vanilla

Cream ingredients together and mix well. Whips up quickly and smoothly with electric beaters. Spread on cake.

QUICK APPLE-BANANA BREAD

½ cup honey
⅓ cup melted butter or oil
½ cup mashed bananas
½ cup applesauce
1 ¼ cups whole-wheat flour
¼ cup soy flour
1 teaspoon baking soda
1 teaspoon baking powder
¼ teaspoon salt
½ teaspoon cinnamon
½ cup chopped nuts (walnuts or peanuts), or ½
*   cup sunflower seeds*
½ cup raisins (optional)

Combine the honey, butter, bananas, and applesauce, and mix well. Combine the other ingredients in a separate bowl and mix well. Put everything together and beat well. Put into a 5″ x 9″ oiled loaf pan, and bake at 350° for 30 to 45 minutes (until a toothpick stuck into the center comes out clean).

BANANA BERRY CREAM

1 cup heavy cream
½ cup orange juice
¼ cup maple syrup
2 bananas
2 cups berries
¼ teaspoon vanilla
¼ teaspoon cinnamon

Whip ½ cup cream in the blender. Pour it into a large bowl. Put the rest of the ingredients (except the remaining cream) into the blender and mix together. Pour this into the whipped cream and fold in. Put this mixture into the freezer and let set for about ½ hour. Remove from the freezer and beat until smooth (can be done in the blender). Whip the remaining ½ cup of cream in the blender and gently fold it into the fruit mixture, so that you make a marbling effect or pattern. Pour this into sherbet or parfait dishes and return them to the freezer. About 20 minutes before serving, remove from the freezer to allow to thaw somewhat, top with fresh berries, or a sprig of mint or toasted almonds.
Serves 6

FRUIT AND YOGURT BUFFET

Yogurt: Plan about ½ to 1 cup per person. Put the yogurt in a serving bowl. To keep it cold, put this bowl inside a larger one that is filled with ice.
Fruit: Plan 1 cup of fruit for every cup of yogurt. Some possibilities are:
  strawberries, blueberries, raspberries
  pitted cherries
  sliced peaches or apples, sprinkled with lemon juice
Honey and maple syrup: Served in small pitchers
Toasted almonds and sunflower seeds
Raisins
Cinnamon

Part Eight

BIBLIOGRAPHY

The Annual Directory of Vegetarian Restaurants, by Loren Kennett Cronk. Daystar Publishing Co., P. O. Box 707, Angwin, California 94508. Invaluable.

Bean Cuisine, by Beverly White. Boston: Beacon Press, 1974. Full of beans.

Beware of the Food You Eat, by Ruth Winter. New York: Crown, 1971.

The Book of Tofu, by William Shurtleff and Akiko Aoyagi. Kanagawa-Ken Japan: Autumn Press, 1975. The authority on tofu.

Bum Steers, by Frances Sheridan Goulart. Old Greenwich, Conn: The Chatham Press, 1975. How to make meatless "meat" from grains.

Chinese Vegetarian Cooking, by Kenneth H. C. Lo. New York: Pantheon Books, 1974.

Common Sense Vegetarianism, by Harry Benjamin. London: Health for All Publishing Co., 1972.

Diet for a Small Planet, by Frances Moore Lappe. New York: Ballantine, 1971. This huge best-seller has influenced millions of people and many other authors, but her main thesis, protein complementing, is overemphasized.

Eating for Life, a Book About Vegetarianism, by Nathaniel Altman. Wheaton, Illinois: The Theosophical Publishing House, 1973.

The Farm Vegetarian Cookbook, edited by Louise Dotzler. Summertown, Tenn: The Book Publishing Co., 1975. Well-written, practical approach to vegan cooking.

500 Recipes for Vegetarian Cookery, by Patty Fisher. London: Hamlyn, 1969.

Great Meatless Meals, by Frances Moore Lappe. New York: Ballantine, 1974. Thirty complete menus with accompanying recipes.

International Vegetarian Cookery, by Sonya Richmond. New York: Arco, 1965. Recipes from many nations adapted to American taste buds.

Laurel's Kitchen: A Handbook for Vegetarian Cookery and Nutrition, by Laura Robertson. Berkeley: Nilgri Press, 1976. Probably the best cookbook on vegetarianism around. Also, a complete guide for vegetarian nutritions.

Modern Vegetarian Cookery, by Walter and Jenny Fliess. Baltimore: Penguin Books, 1964.

A Passion for Vegetables, by Vera Gewanter. New York: Viking, 1980. Recipes from Europe.

Recipes for a Small Planet, by Ellen Buchman Ewald. New York: Ballantine, 1973. A sequel to *Diet for a Small Planet* with more about protein and more recipes.

Recipes for a Longer Life, by Ann Wigmore. Boston: Rising Sun Publications, 1978. Includes a transition diet for beginning vegetarians.

The Soybean Cookbook, by Mildred Lager and Dorothea van Gundy Jones. New York: Arco, 1968. Hundreds of recipes for soybeans.

Tassajara Cooking, by Edward Espe Brown. Berkeley:

Shambhala, 1973. The fundamentals of cooking are covered.

Unmeat: The Case for Vegetarianism, by Stoy Proctor. Nashville: Southern, 1973.

The Vegetarian Epicure, by Anna Thomas. New York: Alfred A. Knopf, 1972. Not for vegans but a very good book for soups and breads.

Vegetarian Gourmet, by Sally and Lucien Berg. New York: McGraw-Hill, 1971. Elaborate meals from all over the world.